PARENTING
PRINCIPLES

"In his book, David Christensen uses his experience as a father and grandfather, and his expertise with teaching through examples and stories, to present a beautifully simple pattern to address the challenges of raising righteous children. I have personally observed this pattern in action and know of the power it can have in families."

—Dr. Craig W. Carver, PhD in Human
Development and Family Science

PARENTING
PRINCIPLES

31 *Teachings* to Raise Children in *Righteousness*

David A. Christensen
author of *Power in Prayer*

CFI
An imprint of Cedar Fort, Inc.
Springville, Utah

ISBN 13: 978-1-4621-1522-8

Published by CFI, an imprint of Cedar Fort, Inc.
2373 W. 700 S., Springville, UT 84663
Distributed by Cedar Fort, Inc., www.cedarfort.com

LIBRARY OF CONGRESS CATALOGING-IN-PUBLICATION DATA

Christensen, David A., 1949- author.
Parenting principles / David A. Christensen.
    pages cm
ISBN 978-1-4621-1522-8 (alk. paper)
1. Parenting--Religious aspects--Church of Jesus Christ of Latter-day Saints. 2. Mormon families. I. Title.

BX8643.F3C47 2015
248.8'45--dc23

2014047639

Cover design by Shawnda T. Craig
Cover design © 2015 Lyle Mortimer
Edited and typeset by Jessica B. Ellingson

Printed in the United States of America

10 9 8 7 6 5 4 3 2 1

Printed on acid-free paper

Contents

Introduction

I REMEMBER YEARS ago sitting around a campfire with a group of priest-age boys. We informally discussed everything from sports and cars to their upcoming senior year. Have you ever been there, discussing and interchanging with boys, or girls, about the great questions of their souls? It's an interesting and important experience. I loved these boys. All of them were as good as they get. They honored their priesthood, they were all leaders in their own right, most were Eagle Scouts, and they were examples in their high school. I would have been happy to have any of my daughters date them.

As the discussion bounced from topic to topic, I posed a question I knew would bring a variety of answers: "So after your missions, what do you guys plan to do with your professional and lives?"

"I plan to study medicine and be a ophthalmologist," answered one.

"I want to work in my dad's construction business and maybe take over when he's ready to retire," responded another.

The high school football star was in the group, and he responded, "Well, I'd love to play ball at BYU and then, with a little luck, play at the professional level like my grandpa did."

Some chatter followed as the other boys extracted more information about the grandfather who had a stint in the NFL. It was then that I noticed a couple of the boys hadn't answered, so I queried, "How about you guys? What do you plan to do with your life?"

There was silence for a moment, and then a deep and simple answer followed from Kent, who was the kind of kid everyone listened to when he spoke. He was a friend to everyone and was respected by all. With a smile and a sense of quiet confidence, he answered, "I'm not sure about my profession yet, but I do know what I want to be when I grow up. All I've ever really wanted to be is a dad—like my dad." There was another quiet moment only interrupted by the call of a loon on the nearby lake and the pop and crackle of the fire.

"Yeah, me too," echoed the football star.

"Yeah, that's right. That's what I want too," said the future ophthalmologist.

That was a teaching moment I couldn't have planned better if I'd tried to engineer and set it up. Our discussion settled into one that lasted for nearly an hour as we sat and talked about dads, the priesthood, providing economically for a family, what they would look for in a potential mother to their children, and preparing for parenthood. Each concluded that what they became in their professional journeys was secondary. It was only important as a support to their primary desire and commitment: to find the right partner, marry her in the temple, and become a parent.

Doctrine from The Church of Jesus Christ of Latter-day Saints on the family is clear. From the early days of the Restoration to the present, the Lord has taught the importance of family and the role of parents. Heavenly Father chastised early leaders with admonitions like, "Inasmuch as parents have children in Zion, or in any of her stakes which are organized, that teach them not, . . . the sin be upon the heads of the parents" (D&C 68:25). Or, "I, the Lord, am not well pleased, . . . for there are idlers among them; and their children are also growing up in wickedness. . . . These things ought not to be" (D&C 68:31–32).

Every latter-day prophet has witnessed and taught the importance of parenthood. Harold B. Lee said, "The most important of the Lord's work you will ever do will be within the walls of our own homes" (*Teachings of Presidents of the Church: Harold B. Lee* [Salt Lake City: The Church of Jesus Christ of Latter-day Saints, 2000], 128–37).

President George Albert Smith taught, "One of the responsibilities of every married couple is to rear a family to the honor and glory of God. . . . Those who follow the customs and habits of the world in preference to that blessing will some day find that all the things they have struggled for are wasted away like ashes, while those who have reared their families to honor God and keep His commandments will find their treasures not altogether here upon the earth in mortality, but they will have their treasures when the celestial kingdom shall be organized on this earth, and those treasures will be their sons and daughters and descendents to the latest generation" (Eric D. Bateman, *The Prophets Have Spoken*, vol. 2 [Salt Lake City: Deseret Book, 2014], 1231–32).

Elder Richard G. Scott reminds us, "One of the greatest blessings we can offer to the world is the power of a Christ-centered home where the gospel is taught, covenants are kept, and love abounds ("For Peace at Home," *Ensign*, May 2013, 30).

The First Presidency made an official declaration to the world that stated, "Husband and wife have a solemn responsibility to love and care for each other and for their children. 'Children are an heritage of the Lord' (Psalm 127:3). Parents have a sacred duty to rear their children in love and righteousness, to provide for their physical and spiritual needs, and to teach them to love and serve one another, observe the commandments of God, and be law-abiding citizens wherever they live. Husbands and wives— mothers and fathers—will be held accountable before God for the discharge of these obligations" ("The Family: A Proclamation to the World," *Ensign*, November 1995, 102).

LDS professionals have supplemented prophetic counsel with reminders and excellent applications, such as Richard and Linda Eyre teach: "Your children are not distractions, they are the very purpose" (Dwight Egan, "Father of 8 Missionary Sons Shares Advice That Helped Him," *Church News*, 9 June 2014, 6).

Hundreds of books are written on the subject. Daily talk shows on TV and the radio discuss parenting philosophies, and almost everyone seems to have an opinion relative to do's and don'ts of discipline and debates how to be a successful parent. Even a cursory online scan of book and article titles remind us that most people struggle with becoming good parents. There is no end of prescriptive solutions for fixing our parenting problems. Just a few titles include: "7 Things You Personally Should Avoid as a Parent," "A Letter to All the People Parenting Right Now," *Love and Logic Magic for Early Childhood, Nurture Shock: New Thinking about Children, The Power of Positive Parenting*, and on and on.

So, why am I—with a few university classes in child development and family relations and four-plus decades of practical experience at parenting—writing a book about parenthood? First, because I was invited to do so. Second, because I know of few things that are more important. I'm like Kent; all I've ever really wanted in my life is to be a good husband and father. I have a testimony of Heavenly Father's plan, and I know He loves me. I know that Jesus is my Savior and that the Holy Ghost will teach me. Key to my critical beliefs is my understanding of the role of prophets, seers, and revelators: to guide, warn, encourage, and inspire us. I consider their teachings fundamental in my attempt to reach my parenting quests.

I have written this book to give short thoughts based on the teachings of a our spiritual leaders. Each chapter will begin with a quote by a prophet, seer, and revelator or a member of the general women's presidencies of the Church. I testify of the value of their perspectives and persuasions. I will then share practical experiences and invite introspection and self-examination. And I will include some scriptural support and conclude with a parting thought.

One of my favorite and most inspiring stories in the Book of Mormon is the brother of Jared being instructed to build barges to cross the sea to the promised land. After completing the barges, he had critical questions regarding the functionality of the vessels: oxygen to breathe and light to see inside. The Lord promptly answered the first question and the problem was remedied.

However, in answer to the second question about light for the vessels, the Lord gave no answer.

The brother of Jared went to work. At great effort, he found ore and created the necessary conditions to process and melt it into the creation of sixteen transparent stones. He then climbed to the mount and fervently prayed to the Lord, explaining that they did not want to travel across the deep in darkness. He meekly and humbly laid the sixteen stones before the Lord. He confessed that, though he had done all he could to find a solution to the issue of darkness inside the barges, these were still just sixteen clear stones.

Then he pleaded, "And I know, O Lord, that thou hast all power, and can do whatsoever thou wilt for the benefit of man; therefore touch these stones, O Lord, with thy finger, and prepare them that they may shine forth in darkness; and they shall shine forth unto us in the vessels which we have prepared, that we may have light while we shall cross the sea" (Ether 3:4).

In essence, he said, "I have done everything I know how to do. And my doings still fall short. The stones I lay before you are just processed ore that represent a lot of work and effort. I know they are just stones. But I know you can make them light. I know that you can touch my doings, as insignificant as they are, and make them the solution to our desires to have light."

The scriptures then state, "And it came to pass that when the brother of Jared had said these words, behold, the Lord stretched forth his hand and touched the stones one by one with his finger" (Ether 3:6).

It is important we believe that the same hand and fingers that touched those stones also touched a few loaves of bread and fishes and made them enough to feed the multitudes. The Lord did that on more than one occasion. It was the same hand and fingers that touched the eyes of the blind and gave them sight. It was that same finger that wrote on the ground before He assured the woman taken in adultery that He did not condemn her and that she should "go, and sin no more" (John 8:11). If we do all that we can do in our mortal power, then it is my testimony that in time or eternity that same loving hand will touch our "doings" and make them enough. If we are seeking, trying, and doing our best to become goodly parents, He will forgive our human errors. We can count on His grace and mercy to set things right.

Throughout the book, I will continually remind us that while there are some principles for parenting, there are no recipes for becoming successful parents. There are simply too many variables. Each child is different. The relationship chemistry is extremely complex in each family situation. There are emotional and mental quotients to consider.

We will look at principles and invite personal examination. We must remember the most important thing we can do as parents is to seek to live worthy of the influence of the Holy Ghost and pay attention to the nudges and direction of the Spirit. As we try our best, we can do as the brother of Jared did and petition the Lord to touch our doings and make them enough.

Nephi's closing words included, "Ye must pray always, and not faint; . . . ye shall pray unto the Father in the name of Christ, that he will consecrate thy performance unto thee, that thy performance may be for the welfare of thy soul" (2 Nephi 32:9). Let's begin.

> Remember: No recipes. Study. Self-examine. Do your best. Live worthy of the Holy Ghost. Pray that the Lord will touch your doings and consecrate them for the blessing and benefit of you, your children, and your grandchildren.

Principle 1 ———————————————————

Parents Who Know

"The responsibility mothers [parents] have today has never required more vigilance. More than at any time in the history of the world, we need mothers [parents] who know. Children are being born into a world where they 'wrestle not against flesh and blood, but against principalities, against powers, against the rulers of the darkness of this world, against spiritual wickedness in high places.' However, mothers [parents] need not fear. When mothers [parents] know who they are and who God is and have made covenants with Him, they will have great power and influence for good on their children." (Julie B. Beck, "Mothers Who Know," *Ensign*, November 2007)

I WAS RECENTLY in a sacrament meeting where one of the eighteen-year-old missionaries was speaking just days before he departed into the mission field. It was a spiritual meeting. Simple in his presence and humble sincerity in his voice, he began his message.

He shared a couple of scriptures, and then he related that his father had taught him important truths associated with the scriptural text he was using. I noted a repeating phrase throughout his heartfelt message: "My dad has taught me" followed by what he had learned from the example and words of his father.

He noted the impact of his father on his own testimony and growth. If that wasn't enough, he said, "Brothers and sisters, my mother's influence in a third grade teaching moment about feeling the Spirit taught me so much." I glanced over at his parents and watched them wipe tears of joy from their eyes. He continued, "I would like to share a journal entry from my grandpa while he was serving as a missionary." As I sat and listened to him quoting his grandfather, my mind drifted from the spoken message to the one

I took away from that meeting: mothers, fathers, and grandparents do make a difference.

I think we all have been impressed with the story in the Book of Mormon about the 2,060 young sons of convert parents who were part of a strategic nonmilitary initiative. But in the end, their role to serve as noncombat decoys in the plan changed surprisingly. They joined the more mature Nephite soldiers and engaged in battle against a more seasoned, mature Lamanite army.

The Nephites were victorious in a this tenuous situation. When body counts were taken of those who had been killed, there was an unbelievable pronouncement. Helaman states,

> And it came to pass that after the Lamanites had fled, I immediately gave orders that my men who had been wounded should be taken from among the dead, and caused that their wounds should be dressed.
>
> And it came to pass that there were two hundred, out of my two thousand and sixty, who had fainted because of the loss of blood; nevertheless, according to the goodness of God, and to our great astonishment, and also the joy of our whole army, there was not one soul of them who did perish; yea, and neither was there one soul among them who had not received many wounds.
>
> And now, their preservation was astonishing to our whole army, yea, that they should be spared while there was a thousand of our brethren who were slain. And we do justly ascribe it to the miraculous power of God, because of their exceeding faith in that which they had been taught to believe—that there was a just God, and whosoever did not doubt, that they should be preserved by his marvelous power.
>
> Now this was the faith of these of whom I have spoken; they are young, and their minds are firm, and they do put their trust in God continually. (Alma 57:24–27)

Perhaps the most impressive point Helaman makes regarding this inspiring story is, "Now they never had fought, yet they did not fear death; and they did think more upon the liberty of their fathers than they did upon their lives; yea, they had been taught by their mothers, that if they did not doubt, God would deliver them. And they rehearsed unto me the words of their mothers, saying: We do not doubt our mothers knew it" (Alma 56:47–48). What a powerful message!

Once following a religion class at BYU–Idaho where I taught and discussed this message, a young woman came up to me after class and said, "Brother Christensen, I know this is a great story about mothers, and I really appreciated your focus on that message. But I want you to know that those boys also had fathers and grandparents." Then she went on to relate how her single father, who had raised his children alone after the untimely death of their mother, had taught them to be faithful. She related how important her grandparents had been in maintaining spiritual stability in their family.

In my experience as a priesthood leader (particularly serving young single adults and missionaries in the field), I have heard on many occasions statements like, "I haven't always had a testimony of the gospel, of Joseph Smith, and the Book of Mormon, but I knew that my dad knew." Or, "For a while I had some doubts, but I knew that my mother knew and had a testimony." Or, "I was challenged by offensive information I discovered on the Internet about the Church, and for a while I wondered and had doubts, but I knew my grandma and grandpa knew it was true."

Yes, the gifts of the Spirit as described in Doctrine and Covenants section 46 are literal: "To some it is given by the Holy Ghost to know that Jesus Christ is the Son of God, and that he was crucified for the sins of the world. To others it is given to believe on their words, that they also might have eternal life if they continue faithful" (verses 13–14).

It behooves us as parents and grandparents to let our children see by example that we *know* what is true. They must never wonder. Parenting includes paying the price to bolster our own testimonies. And we must share them at quiet moments in our homes during family home evening, at bedtime with stories, and in one-on-one moments driving in the car, hiking up a mountain, or lying on a trampoline and looking up at the star-filled sky. A bonus would be that our children hear us publicly bear our testimonies as well.

Parenting Self-Examination

1. If your children or grandchildren were asked to rate your testimony based on their exposure to it, would they be able to say, "I know my parents (or grandparents) know it"? If your testimony is shallow or lacking, what steps can you take to bolster it?
2. What can you do to quietly share your conviction of spiritual truths with your children or grandchildren?
3. Sometimes relationships must be built before testimonies can be effectively shared with children or grandchildren. What can you do this week, and continue in the near future, to build relationships?

Scriptures for Study

| Ephesians 6:10–20 | Moses 5:12 | Nephi 8:37 |
| Alma 56:47–48 | Alma 57:25–27 | D&C 46: 13–14 |

A Parting Thought

Our children and grandchildren need the anchor of strong parents and grandparents who know the truth and live their testimonies. Teaching and demonstrating one's testimony is the order of heaven. The spiritual battles and wars being fought today are far more dangerous and spiritually fatal than the military campaign fought by the 2,060 young men nearly twenty-one centuries ago. Lucifer is engaged in a contest for the souls of our children. Our

Heavenly Father is deeply interested in helping us in our role and responsibility. He will help us win our battles! In the end, we hope to find that, though many may be wounded along the way, not one will have been lost. One of the greatest public honors to be bestowed upon a parent or grandparent is their posterity being able to say, "We do not doubt our parents and grandparents knew it" (see Alma 56:47–48).

> Remember: No recipes. Study. Self-examine. Do your best. Live worthy of the Holy Ghost. Pray that the Lord will touch your doings and consecrate them for the blessing and benefit of you, your children, and your grandchildren.

Principle 2

The Ultimate Laboratory

"A major reason the family is so important to the plan is really quite straightforward: it is the only place where we cannot hide from who we really are as we strive to become what we are destined to become. In essence, a family is the mirror through which we become aware of imperfections and flaws we may not be able or want to acknowledge. No one knows us better than the members of our family. Thus, the family is the ultimate laboratory in mortality for the improving and perfecting of God's children." (David A. Bednar, "'Arise and Shine Forth,'" BYU–Idaho Education Week Devotional, June 28, 2003)

THE LATIN word *laborare* means "labor." From that root, a new word was first used in 1605: *laboratorium*. Laboratory: a place providing for experimentation, observation, and practice. Being a parent and having a family is truly a labor.

It is not a task for the faint-hearted idealist. Neither is it always a blissful fantasyland or imaginary utopia. It is a labor and just plain old hard work.

It is a liberating concept to me to also understand that the home and family is a laboratory. I love knowing that our loving Father in Heaven provided a plan to include a perfect place to exercise our agency in an effort to learn all that needs to be learned in our quest to become like Him. Laboratories are a place where trial and error are acceptable. The very environment of the laboratory encourages practice and experimentation again and again until we can get it right. Even when an occasional explosion occurs, as long as we are trying to learn from our mistakes, it's permissible to clean up the mess and try again to find a better combination, a more suitable approach, and another effective method to bring about desired results.

When we begin our family laboratory, we often think we know how it all works. How many young couples begin their families with preconceived ideas and recipes books of exactly how they will create the ideal family? Their ideas are great and they visualize fantastic outcomes, but someone forgot to mention that—metaphorically speaking—the elements and compounds they learned from the charts didn't include the individual agency of each involved in the experiment, which produce unexpected outcomes. We learn that in this laboratory, the customizing and individualizing role of the Holy Spirit is the critical ingredient.

I know of two such young parents who entered their laboratory desiring as many children as the Lord would give them. There were no two more well-intentioned and better-prepared youngsters in or out of the Church. They sought to do everything right and, by most standards, everything worked out quite well. However, they learned that neither they nor their children were perfect. A time or two, both they and their children had to learn expensive lessons along the way.

During a short chapter of their marathonic efforts to raise

a near-perfect family, one of their children made a series of poor and short-sighted choices that ultimately led to broken hearts and dreams. "How can things ever be right again?" they sorrowed. "What happened?" they wondered. "We have failed," they concluded. In time, they cleaned up the shattered test tubes and broken beakers of the laboratory and followed the Spirit in working on a new experiment, which included their own hearts. They took new approaches and remembered and applied reinforced principles. The child made course corrections and is laboring in a laboratory of his own. The important part of their story includes not only the new heart given to the child but what happened in the hearts of those parents. They have confirmed to each other on many occasions that they learned more about the Atonement and divine grace from that experience in the laboratory than at any other time in their lives. They experienced a multiplicity of tender mercies. Everyone associated with this laboratorial exercise, in the end, has been blessed. What seemed to be a dark abyss has been replaced with hope, light, and deep gratitude.

Yes, when a family is organized, a laboratory is created. We work with one another to increase our understanding, temper impatient attitudes, build faith, repent daily, and forgive seventy times seven as Father in Heaven forgives. We learn to turn the other cheek while becoming more selfless in our desires. We find joy in the journey while learning to take ourselves less seriously. It's pretty hard to fake others out about who we really are when they know us so well. Family members see our private behavior as well as our public display. Duplicity and hypocrisy are exposed in a moment. We come to recognize that we truly do need each other's observations and kindnesses. We practice what we sometimes preach throughout our experiential quest to find the results we hope are pleasing to our Heavenly Father.

Parenting Self-Examination

1. How is the environment in your laboratory? Is everyone involved and on board? Is everyone in agreement to practice, experiment, and find desirable results?

2. Discuss with family members how imperfect people working together within the family unit foster progress. Be sure to include that the critical elements in making the laboratory successful are love, repentance, mercy, forgiveness, and especially the Spirit.

3. Write in your personal journal how you feel about Elder Bednar's quote at the beginning of this chapter.

Scriptures for Study

Proverbs 15:18 ?   Nephi 17:1–3   Mosiah 4:14-15
Alma 34:32–34   D&C 68:25–30

A Parting Thought

It is important to remember that the trial and error of previous laboratories are recorded in the scriptural annals of the past as well as the lives of those who have preceded us. Others have learned a thing or two in their quest that will be valuable to us in ours. We have the experiments of loved ones, the counsel of priesthood leaders, the perspectives of prophets, and most of all, the guidance of the Holy Ghost to assist us in our own laboratories. Someone once said, "If we don't learn from the experiences of others, we are destined to make the same mistakes ourselves." Let us learn from others and apply the principles they've extracted from their experiments while living in such a way that the Holy Ghost can not only guide us through but consecrate our actions for the ultimate good and benefit of all involved.

Remember: No recipes. Study. Self-examine. Do your best. Live worthy of the Holy Ghost. Pray that the Lord will touch your doings and consecrate them for the blessing and benefit of you, your children, and your grandchildren.

Principle 3

Obedience and Discipline

"Parents who fail to teach obedience to their children, if [their] homes do not develop obedience society will demand it and get it. It is therefore better for the home, with its kindliness, sympathy and understanding to train the child in obedience rather than callously to leave him to the brutal and unsympathetic discipline that society will impose if the home has not already fulfilled its obligation." (David O. McKay, *The Responsibility of Parents to Their Children*, 3)

I DON'T KNOW of a more difficult parental responsibility than figuring out how to help each child learn appropriate discipline. James E. Faust once said, "Child rearing is so individualistic. Every child is different and unique. What works with one may not work with another. I do not know who is wise enough to say what discipline is too harsh or what is too lenient except the parents of the children themselves, who love them most. It is a matter of prayerful discernment for the parents. Certainly the overarching and undergirding principle is that the discipline of children must be motivated more by love than by punishment" ("The Greatest Challenge in the World—Good Parenting," *Ensign*, November 1990). Teaching children obedience through kind and consistent discipline is a challenge.

Over the years, my wife and I have studied books written by

knowledgeable professionals on the subject. We have sought to increase our awareness of the theories of discipline and guidance for our children. My undergraduate university study in human development included hours of case studies and extensive consideration of theory. Having eight children of our own required practical application on a daily basis in the laboratory of family life. I've learned that the pursuit of becoming a consistent and loving disciplinarian is certainly not for the faint-hearted or easily fatigued. Teaching obedience and helping a child become self-disciplined is hard work, but it is both necessary and worth the effort.

First, it's important to remember that children come from heaven not only in different sizes and shapes, but also with different attitudes and emotional makeup. Each of our own children manifested different temperaments almost from infancy. I've often thought it would be revealing to informally chat with Lehi and Sariah about the differences in their sons Laman, Lemuel, Sam, and Nephi, who were all born and raised in a common environment. I'd love to know how they'd compare their experience raising their fifth and sixth sons, Jacob and Joseph, whose formative years were in the adversities of the wilderness. Were Laman and Lemuel always disposed to murmuring? Was Sam always inclined toward steadiness? Was Nephi always one to obey? While hearing the full story is impossible, at least in this life, I'm sure they would have many stories to tell. I suspect they would echo my feelings that teaching obedience and disciplining those six boys were challenging and different for each one. Perhaps they would even have a story or two about a challenging stage with Nephi along the way. Those stories might restore hope to us in our battles. I believe children come to earth from the premortal existence with personalities and dispositions. Parents have the task of remembering that.

Second, environment and parental modeling certainly play a role in the process of discipline. What children see, hear, and experience—especially early on in their lives—to some degree impacts their reactions to the boundaries and benefits of discipline. Surely

Lehi and Sariah could share with us the differences in the environment and how it impacted those younger boys.

I am sure that my mother and father struggled with the same issues. Like most, the first half of their nine children were born in pretty economically challenging years. The last half of the family saw better days—a bigger home, nicer automobiles, a swimming pool, a boat, and more nurturing school environments. As stated earlier, each of us came to them with different virtues and vices. Mom and Dad, like all of us, came into parenthood without any experience. They developed their philosophy of parenting based on what they experienced watching their own parents and perhaps in making some conscious decisions to do some things differently. They learned raising my older brothers and sisters and likely adjusted as we younger ones came along. That is a natural process.

I remember when I was a young boy, my dad (a dairy farmer in my early years) taught me a principle or two about his experience with our herd of dairy cows. When I was a young parent, I realized that those principles were the basis for at least some of his philosophy of parenting.

I recall him inviting me to watch cows be put in a new pasture. They would enter the pasture through a gate and would immediately begin to move close to the fence line, checking for breaks or a way to get out. After they inspected the fence and found their new boundary to be secure, they moved out into the center of the pasture to graze. Most of the time they would remain content within the confines of the fence throughout the day until we moved them back into the corral. Over the years, I observed the natural tendency of dairy cows to follow this practice—they were looking for a fence. The fence provided a wonderful and peaceful place to be until they were taken into the corral and made ready for milking.

It was fascinating to see an order to the process when those cows entered the barn to be milked. There were six or eight stalls where the cows were milked while eating some grain. They would line up outside and then enter the barn in the same order two times each day. When we were finished milking one cow, she was released. Her replacement knew it was her turn and always went to the same stall. Consistency and repetition made the process easier.

Dad also taught me that some of the younger heifers or bulls would stay closer to the fence and sometimes test it. There was an instinctive desire to move the boundary. Often they would put their heads through the barbed wire and stretch as far as they could to eat the grass outside of the pasture. If they found a hole or a potential route to freedom, they would often compromise the boundary and get out. During certain seasons, it was almost impossible to keep them in the fence or keep a motivated bull from coming in.

Once, the fence was compromised and later repaired, and we returned the cows to the pasture the next day. Their memories motivated them to look for that same hole and check to see if it was secure. If it was, they would relax and move into the center of the pasture to graze.

Like Dad, I've learned there is a similarity with most children. There is something innate and important about understanding boundaries. Once the boundaries are defined and maintained, then it seems to be a little easier to enjoy life. I've noticed with our children, especially when they were small, that the clear definition of boundaries was an important thing for maintaining a happy and peaceful home. When those boundaries were violated—and they were—there was equally a consistent consequence. How many times at bedtime did we have to put a child back to bed once the boundary of a baby crib was replaced by a "big-people bed"? I know it must have been hundreds of times with one or two of our children. With other children, just a few times, but consistency was the key. Establishing the fence and identifying the boundary is something we as parents are charged with doing.

Shifting boundaries and too many situational holes will cause parents grief in the long run. Giving in by creating a hole in the fence may temporarily stop a tantrum or reduce annoying whining, but it will often cost in the end. When the little tykes find a hole, it's time to fix it and make it secure, not move it.

As children grow older, they learn that the pasture is enlarged, and they anticipate more freedom. They assume their right to roam is automatically expanded. Parents must teach children that these privileges are earned when they demonstrate responsibility and accountability in a smaller arena. When we communicated clear boundaries on small pastures, we found our children later did well in larger ones. Eventually, as youth grow toward young adulthood, they need to learn to position their own boundaries. Self-discipline learned early will serve them well. Giving them practice with fences and boundaries in their childhood will bless them later to establish patterns of self-restraint. They will learn that they can be obedient by choice, not because they are forced to do so. They learn that in direct relationship to the trust and confidence they earn, their power to be self-directed increases.

Please understand that it's important we don't create fourteen-foot chain-link fences with razor wire on top or build our own version of the iron curtain. Boundaries created in love and kindness are different from barriers that do not allow for the exercise of agency. However, if we don't discipline with boundaries now, it's possible that society will impose bars and prison cells to help them learn later.

I am thankful for my dad's barnyard philosophy. It's worked well for us.

Parenting Self-Examination

1. How are the boundaries in your home? Do they teach restraint and reward obedience?

2. Have you created any boundaries that are fuzzy, or are you prone to situational shifting in the fence lines to quiet noisy or negative responses?

3. After all is said and done, what does the Spirit say to you? Do you have any nudges or thoughts to act? Are you willing to pray about it and then take action to do better?

Scriptures for Study

> Proverbs 13:24   Proverbs 23:132   Nephi 4:5
> D&C 121:41

A Parting Thought

Remember, our discussion, and certainly the Lord's instruction through His prophets, is not intended to be discouraging or to make us frustrated. We are all learning as we go. This allows for doing our best and seeking for help from our loving Heavenly Father, whose children we are jointly working with. If your children have gone on to adult pastures and you can see your errors in past judgments in "fence building," take courage and pray that your best efforts will be consecrated for the best good of your children and grandchildren in the long run.

> Remember: No recipes. Study. Self-examine. Do your best. Live worthy of the Holy Ghost. Pray that the Lord will touch your doings and consecrate them for the blessing and benefit of you, your children, and your grandchildren.

Principle 4 ────────────────

Be Certain, Clear, and Consistent

"Our youth want more than landlords. They want people who will love them and lead them. . . . Loving may come naturally, but leading is a polished skill that maybe we don't take seriously enough.

We lead by example more strongly than any other way. That is a heavy burden for parents. . . . If we are to lead in righteousness, there can't be any question where we stand. Small uncertainties on our part can produce large uncertainties in our youth." (Sharon G. Larsen, " 'Fear Not: For They That Be with Us Are More,' " *Ensign*, November 2001)

M om and Dad weren't perfect parents. I'm sure that if they could roll back the clock to the mid 1930s and do it again, they would be just like most of us and undo some things and take a little different approach on others. No, they weren't perfect, but looking back, I can see how perfectly clear Dad was in certain matters. One of those was how we interacted with his bride and sweetheart, our mother. Sassing mother, raising our voices at her, or disrespecting her in any way was a violation of the family code of conduct. He lovingly demanded total respect in the tone and attitude of our voices when we spoke to our mother. There was no uncertainty or lack of clarity in that matter. Any variation in that expectation, at any age, received attention from Dad that spoke volumes. Disrespecting Mother was not tolerated and merited consequences.

With permission of my oldest sister, Carole, I share the following excerpt from her journal regarding one of my earliest memories in our home. I find it to be an ideal illustration of what Sister Larsen may be trying to teach in the above quote.

My sister writes,

> "It's best to get these weeds out while they are small," was Dad's garden advice. "And then," he'd say, "you'll save yourself a lot of work later." He certainly seemed to practice this wise counsel on us as we grew from our seedling state to maturity. An example of this I shall never forget. Dad very rarely spanked us, but when it was necessary, he did not hesitate. I shall be forever grateful that he took the time to destroy the weeds in my life that were capable of choking and binding and preventing my spirit from growing the way it should. This particular "weed

21

pulling" session occurred when I was in my teens. The noxious weeds of disrespect were destroyed by my father before they had even been permitted the chance to take root.

I had been visiting a girl friend. I was sixteen years old with six younger brothers and sisters. I could not help observing the difference in the workload in the homes of my friends where there were only one or two children. My girl friend had only one younger sister. Coming directly from her house, I had an opportunity to instantly compare the difference. I felt picked on and selfishly out of sorts. As I walked in the door, Mother sighed, "Oh, Carole, thank goodness you're home. I need your help. You don't know just how much I need your help!" The silent proclamation of her reasons for needing my assistance was a sink piled high with dirty dishes, bushels of ripe fruit sitting nearby, a fretting baby sister (Lynette) sitting in the high chair, toys strewn about underfoot with little brothers David and Marvin in the middle of them, and a huge pile of clean laundry on the table waiting to be folded. I knew she had been gathering the harvest from our large garden, and I could smell bread baking. Inwardly I knew the day had been an extra busy one for her, but my compassion remained submerged in my selfishness, and I lashed out at her in cutting tones: "Oh, I hate it! I hate it! I hate it! All you think I'm good for is work, work, work! My friends don't have to be slaves like me. I hate it all!"

My own spiteful words surprised me and sounded foreign and unreal and terribly daring and crude. Not until that moment did I realize that Dad was home. It was the height of bad manners in our home to be sassy, hateful, or disrespectful, especially to our parents. I heard his footsteps, loud and heavy, as he approached me from the adjoining room. He grabbed my arm and firmly turned me over his knee, and then he spanked me . . . hard! He stood me up, looked me straight in the eye, and said, "Young lady, don't you ever, *ever* speak to your mother in that tone of voice again!"

My brothers and sisters stood there as wide-eyed and frightened witnesses to the scene. He turned to them and sternly informed them, "And that goes for the rest of you too!" He marched out of the room in long angry strides. My emotions welled up inside. I knew I had deserved that. I was really shaken at the moment, temporarily feeling humiliated and brought down, and yet somewhere inside of me was a feeling that said, "I'm glad I didn't get away with that." Never again did I speak to my mother that way. I am grateful I do not have to regret cutting words or disrespectful actions toward my sweet mother. Those weeds were quickly destroyed by a loving, caring father, and that episode has stood as a well learned lesson for me by a father who loves and respects my mother and who I know loves and respects me. Often in later years, my father and I have laughed together as we remembered "the spanking." I continue to be proud of my father for always loving and respecting my mother. Thank goodness he cared enough for me to quickly pull those weed seedlings in my life before they had a chance to grow and bring unhappiness to me and to those I love. (Carole C. Mathews, "Green Fields," *Patchwork*, 1980–81, 3–4)

I'm grateful for a dad who led by example and boldly communicated with clarity in this particular matter. I have to believe my dad and mother didn't agree on all matters, but Dad practiced what he preached and expected of us. I do not ever remember him speaking in a cross or angry voice to Mom. His actions and respect for Mother spoke louder than his words and were more convincing than a rare spanking like my sister Carole received.

Dad never forced Church attendance, but it was clear that we were expected to be ready to go and in the car a half hour before the meeting was to start. Guess what? He was too. We understood that we each had a short list of chores, which were not negotiable. It was not complicated to understand that we were expected to do our best in school regardless of the grade we received. There was zero ambiguity in whether or not we were to live the standards of the Church in our daily lives. In general, while some matters deserved flexibility, there were some that were planted firmly in our understanding. There were no shifting or sandy interpretations.

Parenting Self-Examination

1. What are the core matters in your home and family relationships? Is there clarity of understanding by family members regarding what they are?
2. Is there any need to reestablish those core matters or reduce ambiguity in the interpretation of them?
3. Is there any need to repent or change?

Scriptures for Study

Proverbs 29:182	Nephi 31:9–10	Alma 17:11
Thessalonians 3:92	Alma 39:11	Timothy 4:11–12

A Parting Thought

I am so grateful that Dad intuitively understood and applied the concept Sister Larsen teaches: "If we are to lead in righteousness, there can't be any question where we stand. Small uncertainties on our part can produce large uncertainties in our youth." Whether Dad approached perfection as a parent or not, the certainty, clarity, and consistency in core matters has blessed my life and the lives of my eight brothers and sisters and their posterity.

Remember: No recipes. Study. Self-examine. Do your best. Live worthy of the Holy Ghost. Pray that the Lord will touch your doings and consecrate them for the blessing and benefit of you, your children, and your grandchildren.

Principle 5 ————————————————————

Prophetic Promises

"We, as members of The Church of Jesus Christ of Latter-day Saints, must stand up to the dangers which surround us and our families. To aid us in this determination, I offer several suggestions. . . . I begin with family home evening. We cannot afford to neglect this heaven-inspired program. It can bring spiritual growth to each member of the family, helping him or her to withstand the temptations which are everywhere. The lessons learned in the home are those that last the longest." (Thomas S. Monson, "Constant Truths for Changing Times," *Ensign*, May 2005)

I HONESTLY CAN'T remember when my parents became consistent in having family home evening, but I do recall how important it was in our home while I was growing up. About the time my father was born, the First Presidency of the Church gave an official statement. My grandparents no doubt heard and followed the counsel given when the First Presidency said, "To this end we advise and urge the inauguration of a 'home evening' throughout the Church, at which time fathers and mothers may gather their boys and girls about them in the home and teach them the word of the Lord. . . . If the Saints obey this counsel, we promise that great blessings will result. Love at home and obedience to parents will increase. Faith will be developed in the hearts of the youth of Israel, and they will gain power to combat the evil influences and temptations which beset them" ("Family Home Evening: Counsel and a Promise," *Ensign*, June 2003; published in *Improvement Era*, June 1915, 733–34).

Wow! That is a significant promise to parents and families. In the mid-1970s, in an informal setting, another prophet, seer, and revelator instructed members of our stake that if we would religiously and consistently hold our family home evenings, the power of Satan would not prevail long term with our children, and they would be inclined toward living the gospel and keeping their covenants. He further stated that if our children did stray, it would only be for a season. He assured us that the power of love would reach out and bring our children back to the home and the gospel. We determined that we would embrace that promise and bind the Lord to that promise. Not all of our family home evenings have been five-star evenings, and we've had our share of casual and simple gatherings. But we can say that on the majority of Monday evenings, we could be found convening together for an opening prayer, singing, family business, a gospel lesson, an activity of some sort, a kneeling family prayer, and always refreshments. It's just become a way of life in our home.

Some evenings, usually monthly, have been reserved as "Grand Family Home Evening" when extended family gathers following a similar format of music, a lesson, and always a special dessert. Other times, we share the evening with friends and neighbors. We had a monthly interview night. Each of the children had one-on-one personal time with Dad to talk about goals, challenges, and anything they wanted to talk about. While I did that, my wife participated in activities at the kitchen table or on the living room floor with the others waiting for their turn. Another family home evening tradition was school blessings the Monday evening before school starts. We sat together as each child received a father's blessing to help them through the school year. As always, we finished with refreshments. Elder Carlos Asay taught, "All of these are important and have their place. However, the participation in such performances and the reporting of such activity must not become the end. They are means of involving, means of teaching, and means of blessing people. All should be engaged in for the purpose of saving and exalting souls" ("Parent-Child Interviews," *Ensign*, November 1983). It's all about saving and exalting the soul—and always having refreshments at the end.

26

I have a personal testimony that the Lord has kept His promise. I have seen that as we and the extended family have obeyed the counsel to set apart Monday evening for family, great blessings have resulted. We have seen love at home, and obedience to parents has increased. I'm a great believer in following the counsel of our prophets, seers, and revelators. Blessings attend prophetic promises.

Outside of simple obedience to counsel and expecting the associated blessings from following prophets, I've wondered at times what it is about family home evening that causes such positive results. In our family, I'm sure singing was not anything that brought down the powers of heaven—we don't have extraordinary talent. Family calendar coordination and business definitely weren't it, though they helped everyone know what was going on in each others' lives. It likely wasn't the activities—most of them were kind of corny. The gospel discussions, because of the broad age range of our children, weren't particularly edifying to both the older and younger children every week. Our opening and closing prayers were consistent, but depending on which member of the family prayed, they were short and fairly routine. I've concluded that all those things have contributed to the storehouse of blessings given to us for having our family home evenings—and the popcorn, brownies, cookies, gallons of ice cream, and carmeled apples helped too. But it was more about being together and enjoying each other in moments of sweet reverence, fun, and laughter, and always having dessert or refreshments, which concluded our dedicated family time with pleasantness. Happy times!

Parenting Self-Examination

1. How are you doing with family home evenings in your family? Is there a sense of tradition and consistency in the weekly dedicated time together?

2. What can you do to enhance your family time together? What

can you do to be more consistent? Depending on your situation in life, solicit family support for improving the quality and perhaps quantity of family home evenings.

3. If you've been blessed by family home evenings, send someone in your family a handwritten note thanking them for making it a priority. If you feel lacking in the area of family home evenings, write someone a note inviting them to engage with you in "stepping it up" and becoming better at following prophetic counsel and seeking for the associated blessings.

Scriptures for Study

Deuteronomy 7:9   2 Corinthians 1:20   Ephesians 4:14
Hebrews 10:35–36   D&C 21:4–6   D&C 1:38

A Parting Thought

I've learned that there are many good families in the Church and around the world who have not embraced family home evening as a functioning part of their family life. As previously stated, heaven will attest that some of our family home evenings (now well over two thousand) were going through the motions. I simply have a feeling that all of our attempts to follow prophetic counsel, even though they were sometimes an exercise in frustration, have contributed to having children and an ever-growing number of grandchildren who expect to have and enjoy family home evening every week. I recommend the practice and have a testimony of the promises given by prophets to those who will listen.

Remember: No recipes. Study. Self-examine. Do your best. Live worthy of the Holy Ghost. Pray that the Lord will touch your doings and consecrate them for the blessing and benefit of you, your children, and your grandchildren.

Principle 6 ———————————————

Just Love Them

"There is no one perfect way to be a good mother. Each situation is unique. Each mother has different challenges, different skills and abilities, and certainly different children. The choice is different and unique for each mother and each family. Many are able to be 'full-time moms,' at least during the most formative years of their children's lives, and many others would like to be. Some may have to work part- or full-time; some may work at home; some may divide their lives into periods of home and family and work. What matters is that a mother loves her children deeply and, in keeping with the devotion she has for God and her husband, prioritizes them above all else." (M. Russell Ballard, "Daughters of God," *Ensign*, May 2008)

I T IS easy to be inspired by one of my personal favorite stories in the Book of Mormon: Helaman's two thousand stripling warriors. This is not the only time I refer to it, because it has multiple tender applications. Mormon, quoting from Helaman's account of his association with these young men, provides a backdrop for making one of his several points by saying, "And they were all young men, and they were exceeding valiant for courage, and also for strength and activity; but behold, this was not all— they were men who were true at all times in whatsoever thing they were entrusted. Yea, they were men of truth and soberness, for they had been taught to keep the commandments of God and to walk uprightly before them" (Alma 53:20–21). "And I did remember the words which they said unto me that their mothers had taught them" (Alma 57:21).

Since there were eventually 2,060 of these young men, it is safe to say that there were 2,060 ways that these saintly mothers executed their roles in raising their sons. They were all convert mothers. Some were with their husbands and others were likely single, having lost their companions in pre-conversion war encounters. We can only speculate the composition and nature of their circumstances, but we can be sure that, like mothers and fathers today, their respective situations varied. In your circles of family and friends, you undoubtedly know single parents whose former spouses have wavered, while others go it alone because of an untimely death. Hence it follows that you know fathers who must also act as mothers and mothers as fathers while they move alone through this season. You likely know others who have to support their spouses or a special child in matters of ill health or disability. Many situations require that both parents dedicate themselves to full-time employment outside of the home. In short, for every child in every family, circumstances, personality, and other dynamics make each parent-child relationship just a little different. I believe that the parents of the 2,060 young men were much the same.

So what was the common denominator in their philosophies of raising children that penetrated the varied circumstances, which in the end produced results so notable that we refer to this story as a standard today? What did they do that yielded children so powerful that it was said, "And we do justly ascribe it to the miraculous power of God, because of their exceeding faith in that which they had been taught to believe—that there was a just God, and whosoever did not doubt, that they should be preserved by his marvelous power. Now this was the faith of these of whom I have spoken; they are young, and their minds are firm, and they do put their trust in God continually" (Alma 57:26–27).

Two men (brothers-in-law) in their early sixties sat in a local Costa Vida restaurant, one enjoying his smothered sweet pork burrito while the other bit into a stuffed green chili chicken quesadilla. "Thanks for inviting me to dinner tonight," said John. "It's been a lonely week of leftovers and scrounge-abouts since Linda's been gone." Tom agreed heartily and added, "This is the third time I've been here this week, and I might be back a time or two next, depending when Sherri decides to come home." John's wife was in Denver helping their daughter and young family pack boxes and load a self-moving van because they were relocating to start a new job in Santa Fe, New Mexico. Sherri was in El Segundo helping their daughter, just home from the hospital with their new baby girl, and would be occupied in corralling and entertaining the baby's two rambunctious brothers aged two and four while Mom and infant settled in.

"Linda is one who just has to be helping the kids however she can, even though they're all pretty self-sufficient," mused John. "She's always been that way since the kids were small. She's always helping them." Then he enumerated a fraction of the many ways his bride of forty-two years had loved and served her kids over the years:

- Her home was always a place where her kids could bring their friends, and they would always eat something. She cooked her way into their hearts.
- She played with her kids, whether it was dolls, soccer, toy cars, or a tea party with dress up clothes.
- She lead a quilt tying party for the kids or showed them how to make simple clothes for their stuffed animals.
- The library and book mobile was a place she and her kids visited, reading to them when they were younger and listening to them when they got older.
- Walking in the fall leaves, winter snow, spring rain, and summer sun was something she always found time and energy to do.
- Taking each child on a one-on-one shopping date where they could not overspend on anything, but they had to spend every penny of whatever was budgeted.

"Sherri's the same way!" Tom quipped with a chuckle in his voice. "She decided just before our first, Nate, was born that she would place her diploma and her job on the shelf until our kids were all out of school." Then he went on to explain, smiling all the time, "What she didn't realize was that her first baby would have a baby before her last baby graduated from high school." Chuckling with a tinge of pride, he said, "Now, twenty-four grandbabies later, I'm eating leftovers, Wendy's salads, an occasional Big Mac, and sweet pork burritos like this." He point to his plate. "The diploma and job are still on the shelf." Getting a little more serious, he added his own short list of ways that Sherri manifested her love for her children:

- In everything she did as a mother, she created smells, sounds, and sights that would endear the kids' hearts to home.
- She put quotes from prophets all over the house on walls, mirrors, and doors, and even tucked them into their shirt pockets or clean, folded clothing.
- She made sure there were plenty of books on the library shelf that could be referenced in moments when her kids needed answers to questions.
- She loved to be a "taxi mom" because it gave her time to hold them captive while she checked their spiritual temperature and they told jokes or talked.
- She watched every episode of *Anne of Green Gables* with her girls multiple times while eating liquorice.
- When the kids talked to her, she looked at her children in the face as if she needed to lip-read, listening with her eyes as well as with her ears.

John was eating the last bite of his quesadilla when he stopped, looked at his brother-in-law Tom, and said, "Are we glad we married these girls or what? It hasn't always been easy being married to a woman who would rather be with our kids and grandkids," he paused momentarily, "and me too most of the time. But I wouldn't have it any other way." Tom agreed, nodding his head affirmatively. "Yep. As we've been talking here tonight, I've realized that between us, we have eleven children and about forty grandkids.

Except for a short challenging glitch in a couple of their lives, they're all 100 percent turning out nicely, don't you think?"

"I'm full. I think I'll take my dessert and eat it tomorrow. I've got a few more days alone," Tom said. Just as they exited the restaurant, John turned to Tom and said, "Linda gets back tomorrow, so we'll have you over to eat before Sherri gets back." The two parted, each to their cars in the crowded parking lot.

John and Tom had come to understand that mothers are primarily responsible for the nurture of their children. No wonder in the aforementioned story of the 2,060 young men that the mothers were the ones their leaders "ascribed," and the boys themselves credited their mothers as the influence on their faith and ultimate miracle of preservation of their lives.

Effective mothers remember and recognize that the joys of parenthood come in moments. From the day Adam and Eve were expelled from the Garden, the experience of parenting came with hard and frustrating times. It is important that we as fathers and mothers remember that joys, satisfactions, and the good that we can do come in moments. Spontaneous opportunities are often more impactful than planned experiences.

Author Anna Quindlen said, "The biggest mistake I made [as a parent] is the one that most of us make. . . . I did not live in the moment enough. This is particularly clear now that the moment is gone, captured only in photographs. There is one picture of [my three children] sitting in the grass on a quilt in the shadow of the swing set on a summer day, ages six, four, and one. And I wish I could remember what we ate, and what we talked about, and how they sounded, and how they looked when they slept that night. I wish I had not been in such a hurry to get on to the next thing: dinner, bath, book, bed. I wish I had treasured the "doing" a little more and the "getting it done" a little less" (*Loud and Clear* [New York City: Ballantine Books, 2004], 10–11).

There are so many good things with which to fill our children's lives: music lessons, baseball practice, day camps, soccer games, dance, and Scouts, to name a few. Mothers can or may need to be involved in full- or part-time employment, fitness lessons, study groups, PTA, or school support groups, and we haven't even mentioned all there is to do in the Church programs, callings, and helping others in time of need.

With all there is to do, and as challenging as it is to be a good parent, we must pray deeply and humbly about our roles. It is critical we remember that we are jointly involved with the parent of us all—Heavenly Father. He loves us and He loves His other children who we are jointly raising. As we endeavor to live our lives in such a way that we qualify for the direction of the Holy Ghost, we will do just fine.

It would be interesting if we could line up a sampling of twenty of those mothers of the 2,060 young men and ask them the question, "Sisters, you are and have been motherhood heroes to millions through the years. You are incredible examples to be sure, but the record doesn't state exactly what you did to produce such wonderful young men. What did you do?" I believe that they would all humbly and quietly reply with some form of, "Oh, we don't think we did anything special. The Lord blessed us with good kids, and we can't take any credit for that." If we pressed them further, I suggest they would likely conclude with, "We loved them. We loved God and we loved them."

Parenting Self-Examination

1. What can you do to declutter your life so that you can nurture your children with love?
2. Set aside a few minutes and attempt to take a look through your children's eyes about how frequently and deeply they perceive and feel that you love them. Then make a time for them individually and ask them, "Do you know that I love you?" Follow that with, "When can you feel that I love you?" The discussion might gravitate to, "How can I improve?"

3. If you are a single parent, you are likely necessarily engaged in full- or part-time employment. How are you investing your early mornings, evenings, and weekends in ways to foster opportunities for creating loving moments? How can you do better?

Scriptures for Study

Psalm 127:3–5	Titus 2:4–8	Luke 15:20
1 Corinthians 13:4–8	Ephesians 6:14	Alma 53:20–21
Alma 57:21	Alma 13:28	D&C 12:8

A Parting Thought

Love is the most powerful conduit for teaching our children. They will not always agree or be as obedient as we wish, but if they know in their hearts that we love them, they will be responsive (over time) to the desires of our hearts. Whether you are married, divorced, working, serving, or leading, Heavenly Father loves you and your children. We will not be left alone. We will be inspired. Elder Ballard testifies, "What matters is that a mother loves her children deeply and, in keeping with the devotion she has for God and her husband, prioritizes them above all else."

Remember: No recipes. Study. Self-examine. Do your best. Live worthy of the Holy Ghost. Pray that the Lord will touch your doings and consecrate them for the blessing and benefit of you, your children, and your grandchildren.

Principle 7

Honoring Mother

"Many years ago the First Presidency issued a statement that has had a profound and lasting influence upon me. 'Motherhood,' they wrote, 'is near to divinity. It is the highest, holiest service to be assumed by mankind. It places her who honors its holy calling and service next to the angels.' Because mothers are essential to God's great plan of happiness, their sacred work is opposed by Satan, who would destroy the family and demean the worth of women." (Russell M. Nelson, "Our Sacred Duty to Honor Women," *Ensign*, May 1999)

As I write this, there is a conference going on in Aspen, Colorado, designed to consider ideas and issues that impact the world. One of the issues being discussed is the question regarding whether or not women can "have it all." Meaning, is it possible to have prestige and worldly success in the business world or the political arena while being successful as a mother and homemaker? Bubbling out of that forum, I picked up the following online news report that told the story of Indra Nooyi. She had learned that Pepsi was going to make her its president, so she went home early to share the exciting news with her family. Before she could tell them, her mother sent her out to get milk. Nooyi's husband had been home for hours and the family employed several housekeepers, but she went out and bought the milk. When she got home, she slammed the carton on the counter.

> Finally spitting out news of her promotion and balking at the errand, Nooyi's mother remained nonplussed. "Let me explain something to you," Nooyi recalls her saying. "You might be president of PepsiCo. You might be on the board of directors. But when you enter this house, you're the wife, you're the daughter, you're the daughter-in-law, you're the mother. You're

all of that. Nobody else can take that place. So leave that . . . crown in the garage."

This exchange typifies the elusive balance between career and motherhood that she still struggles to navigate every day, Nooyi said. . . .

"Motherhood is a full-time job. Being a CEO of a company is three full-time jobs rolled into one," she said. "How can you do justice to it all?"

Having been married for thirty-four years with two daughters, Nooyi says she has concluded that women simply can't have it all. "If you ask our daughters, I'm not sure they will say that I've been a good mom," she conceded. (Geoff Weiss, "Pepsi CEO Indra Nooyi: 'I Don't Think Women Can Have It All,'" Entrepreneur.com, July 2, 2014)

I contrast that article and the national debate regarding the war on women with my recollection of a great woman in my life. On July 6, 1917, in a remote town in northern Arizona, it was raining. The summer monsoon season produced thunder, lightning, and rain. A flash of lightning followed by thunder accompanied the rainwater dripping from the overhead canvas of May Whiting Cardon's bed while she gave birth to my mother. In Gilbert, Arizona, ninety-five years later, I sat by Mother's bedside, holding her hand. Four of my siblings circled her bed with a large group of grandchildren and great-grandchildren looking on. The little room was crowded while we sang hymns in harmony to comfort her through unconsciousness and labored breathing. Outside that little bedroom were another three children, sixty-plus grandchildren, and over a hundred great-grandchildren, who, knowing of her failing health, affectionately awaited news of her passing. Coincidentally (or maybe not), the late summer monsoons had again produced a storm—thunder and lightening attended the scene. But this time Mom was in the security of a comfortable home. Shortly after midnight on September 11, 2012, just as a rumble of thunder followed a flash of lightning outside, Mom took her last breath and exited mortality. On the other side of the veil, a husband, parents, brothers, sisters, two children, and three grand-children awaited her with equal love and celebration of her life.

I love the following quote by Sister Marjorie Hinckley:

> I don't want to drive up to the pearly gates in a shiny sports car, wearing beautifully tailored clothes, my hair expertly coiffed, and with long, perfectly manicured fingernails. I want to drive up in a station wagon that has mud on the wheels from taking kids to scout camp. . . . I want to be there with a smudge of peanut butter on my skirt from making sandwiches for a sick neighbor's children. I want to be there with a little dirt under my fingernails from helping to weed someone's garden. I want to be there with children's sticky kisses on my cheeks and the tears of a friend on my shoulder. I want the Lord to know I was really here and that I really lived. (Virginia H. Pearce, *Glimpses into the Life and Heart of Marjorie Pay Hinckley* [Salt Lake City: Deseret Book, 1999])

She never voiced it, but Mom always felt the same. She was first and foremost a mother who loved her children and any other who was without the heart and care of their own mother. To some, the tasks associated with showing her love for us could be counted as menial. Cooking, washing, mending, and always giving didn't detract from her focus.

I don't in any way want to discount or diminish the extraordinary contributions made by women in the corporate world, politics, education, medicine, and law. A long list can be made of women who have shaped and influenced the destiny of us all and put a significant mark on the world. We should, and I do, applaud them for all contributions, insights, and life-changing gifts. But motherhood, as Elder Nelson reminds us, "is near to divinity. It is the highest, holiest service to be assumed by mankind. It places her who honors its holy calling and service next to the angels."

Elder Neal A. Maxwell adds,

When the real history of mankind is fully disclosed, will it feature the echoes of gunfire or the shaping sounds of lullabies? The great armistices made by military men or the peacemaking of women in homes and in neighborhoods? Will what happened in cradles and kitchens prove to be more controlling than what happened in congresses? When the surf of the centuries has made the great pyramids so much sand, the everlasting family will still be standing, because it is a celestial institution, formed outside telestial time. The women of God know this. ("The Women of God," *Ensign*, May 1978)

Parenting Self-Examination

1. Earning the respect and admiration of being a mother takes work and consistency. What can you do to merit the respect? What can you do to show your love and respect to women and mothers in your life?

2. Who do you know that seems to understand the role of motherhood? Find a way to talk with them about what they've learned along the way that can help you keep the eternal perspective as taught by the First Presidency: "Motherhood is near to divinity. It is the highest, holiest service to be assumed by mankind. It places her who honors its holy calling and service next to the angels."

3. Since motherhood is so important, we can expect Satan to discount it and distract men and women from honoring the role. Can you see or feel Satan's subtle influence planting seeds in your own heart that discount motherhood? If so, what can you do to combat the feelings? If not, what are you doing to guard against the tide of the world that supports Satan's view?

Scriptures for Study

Exodus 20:12	Proverbs 1:7–9	Proverbs 31:28
Deuteronomy 5:16	Matthew 15:4–5	Alma 53:20–21

A Parting Thought

From conception, the beat of our mothers' hearts will always be with us in some way. May we express our love to our mothers, wives, sisters, and daughters. I conclude with Elder Nelsons invitation: "Express your love to your wife, to your mother, and to the sisters. Praise them for them for their forbearance with you even when you are not at your best. Thank the Lord for these sisters who—like our Heavenly Father—<u>love us not only for what we are but for what we may become</u>" ("Our Sacred Duty to Honor Women," *Ensign*, May 1999). I am eternally grateful for my mother, for my wife—who is the light of my life—for six daughters, for two daughters-in-law, and for a special, unofficially adopted friend who all have blessed my life.

Remember: No recipes. Study. Self-examine. Do your best. Live worthy of the Holy Ghost. Pray that the Lord will touch your doings and consecrate them for the blessing and benefit of you, your children, and your grandchildren.

Principle 8

Teaching about Work

" 'In the sweat of thy face shalt thou eat bread' is not outdated counsel. It is basic to personal welfare. <u>One of the greatest favors parents can do for their children is to teach them to work</u>. Much has been said over the years about children and monthly allowances, and opinions and recommendations vary greatly. I'm from the 'old school.' I believe that children should earn their money needs through service and appropriate chores. I think it is unfortunate for a child to grow up in a home where the seed is planted in the child's mind that there is a family money tree that automatically drops 'green stuff' once a week or once a month." (Marvin J. Ashton, "One for the Money," *Ensign*, September 2007)

D AVID, WOULD you be willing to stay home from school tomorrow and help me and Grandpa Christensen build a new barn?" Dad asked me one evening just before bed in the fall of 1959. His request was a definite deviation from his usual stance that if we could breathe, we needed to be at school—sick or not. Naturally, I could think of no good reason to decline the invitation, and so I answered affirmatively.

What was my dad thinking? When I reflect on that day, it strikes me that Dad (who I knew could build anything by himself) would ask his nine-year-old skinny son and my aging eighty-four-year-old grandpa to help him build a simple but suitable barn in a single day. Grandpa was bright of mind but shuffled slowly about and I suspect was a greater liability than an asset. Though willing, I was young, inexperienced, and a potential weak link in getting the job done. There were holes to dig, posts to bury, framework to erect, barn wood to nail, and a tin roof to lay. Well, I wasn't great with a shovel yet, I had little understanding of structural sound-ness, and I was certainly limited in my ability to effectively drive nails or manage large sheets of corrugated roofing metal. I don't know how effective Grandpa was in his contribution, but I imag-ine my level of assistance was lacking. But I remember that experi-ence like it was yesterday. Staying home from school to work with my dad and grandpa in erecting a structure that I would see almost every day for the next eight years (and continue to remember in excess of half century). I felt like I was needed and appreciated. How I enjoyed that day!

Dad was a dairy farmer turned contractor, and work was something all of us learned to do. When I was five and six years old, I tended to helping with the chickens on our egg farm, feed-ing calves, sweeping the barn floor, and other duties. But on that particular day in the fall of 1959, what was my dad really trying to accomplish? Why would he keep me home from school to help out on the new barn? It was not for my skilled "assistance" or shear strength. To answer the question, let's consider prophetic instruction and insight.

> "To teach our children to work is a primary duty of parenthood. Our children have experienced unprecedented prosperity created by parents who have worked hard to provide what they themselves did not have as youngsters. If we are to save our children temporally and spiritually, we must train them to work. They must learn by example that work is not drudgery, but a blessing." (J. Richard Clarke, "The Value of Work," *Ensign*, May 1982)

> "We want you parents to create work for your children." (Spencer W. Kimball, *Teachings of Presidents of the Church: Spencer W. Kimball* [Salt Lake City: The Church of Jesus Christ of Latter-day Saints, 226], 114–23)

> "Work is honorable. Developing the capacity to work will help you contribute to the world in which you live. . . . It will bless you and your family, both now and in the future. Learning to work begins in the home. Help your family by willingly participating in the work necessary to maintain a home. . . . Set high goals for yourself, and be willing to work hard to achieve them." ("Work and Self-Reliance," *For the Strength of Youth*, 40–41)

> "For me, work became a joy when I first worked alongside my father, grandfather, uncles, and brothers. I am sure that I was often more of an aggravation than a help, but the memories are sweet and the lessons learned are valuable." (James E. Faust, "The Greatest Challenge in the World—Good Parenting," *Ensign*, November 1990, 32–35)

I can only surmise that Dad wasn't as concerned about

building a barn as he was about raising a boy. It was less about my capabilities and more about creating capacities: a joy for work and personal association. The barn was just an excuse. I marvel and note that he conveniently seized that day to also bridge generations and form memories to last a lifetime. Grandpa died just a couple of years later, but the memories of me working with him and Dad will stay with me forever.

You may not have a barn to build, but you can find similar excuses to build a boy or girl and maybe even bridge the generation. We can all find ways to create "work" that will increase capacities in our children and grandchildren. It may be appropriate to pay them for their services, but don't make the mistake of making remuneration the focus. Remember: work, association, conversation, enjoyment, accomplishment, and, above all, memories are the objectives.

Parenting Self-Examination

1. How are you doing in your duty of teaching your children to find joy in work?
2. Make a short list of opportunities or excuses available to you to find work for your children. Decide how you will use those opportunities to create enjoyable experiences to foster a love for work.
3. Are there generational bridges that can be integrated into your work plans?

Scriptures for Study

| Proverbs 13:11 | Matthew 25:14–30 | Moses 5:1 |
| 1 Thessalonians 4:11 | Mosiah 10:4–5 | D&C 107:99–100 |

A Parting Thought

I suppose it could be debated whether a parent should take a child out of school to work on a barn. Sometimes finding meaningful jobs is not easy and can be viewed as using children to reduce the menial work of parents. The subject of allowances can always bring some lively discussion in parental circles. However, in my mind, the principle given in "The Family: A Proclamation to the World" is basic to the parental charge to teach our children to enjoy work: "Successful marriages and families are established and maintained on principles of faith, prayer, repentance, forgiveness, respect, love, compassion, *work*, and wholesome recreational activities" (*Ensign*, November 1995, 102; emphasis added).

Should be every family's focus/motto

Remember: No recipes. Study. Self-examine. Do your best. Live worthy of the Holy Ghost. Pray that the Lord will touch your doings and consecrate them for the blessing and benefit of you, your children, and your grandchildren.

Principle 9

A Foundation of Love

"Parenting is not only challenging, but it provides life's greatest joys. . . . Love is the foundational virtue in building a strong home. Our Father in Heaven exemplifies the pattern we should follow. He loves us, teaches us, is patient with us, and entrusts us with our agency. . . . Discipline, which means 'to teach,' is confused with criticism. Children—as well as people of all ages—improve behavior from love and encouragement more than from fault-finding. . . . We demonstrate our love for family members not only in teaching them affirmatively but also in giving them of our time." (Susan W. Tanner, "Did I Tell You . . . ?" *Ensign*, May 2003)

TELLING OUR children that we love them is one thing. Making sure they feel it in their hearts is entirely another. President Hinckley said, "Love can make the difference—love generously given in childhood and reaching through the awkward years of youth. . . . And encouragement that is quick to compliment and slow to criticize" ("Bring Up a Child in the Way He Should Go," *Ensign*, November 1993, 60). Identifying the faults and criticizing our children significantly discounts the "I love you" phrases we speak with our lips, heartfelt or not.

I think it's safe to say that most of us as parents fall into the trap of identifying faults and preaching to our children. Because we love them, we want to help them fix their shortcomings and failings and measure up to higher standards or more appropriate behaviors. The motive to facilitate improvement is good, but the approach may fail to move our sincere "I love you" into the minds and hearts of our children. So how can we help our children to overcome their imperfections and misdeeds without pointing them out? How can we demonstrate our love and confidence?

My parents told me frequently that they loved me. Expressions of love were bounteous in our home. There was no question about their love for us. We all knew it. However, like most parents, Mom and Dad knew how to identify our shortcomings as well. "Your room is messy." "Your grades don't show you're working hard enough." "You are planning to be late. Why did you sleep in?" "Clean up after yourself." But my parents also had informal techniques they were absolutely masterful at to build us up. In explaining their style, let me first use a life experience metaphor for context.

Many years ago, a good man initiated a change in my life. I was cut from my tenth grade high school basketball team. My expectations were shattered! In my immature teenage mind, I was one of the fifty losers who didn't make it. I did not measure up to the expectations of significant adults in my life. In an effort to mend my broken heart, my dad suggested I could play Church ball. I was not comforted by that suggestion. I didn't want to play Church basketball. I wanted to play high school varsity basketball, be one of the best, make the all-state team, get a college scholarship, and maybe even play in the NBA. Church basketball leagues, in my mind at that tender age, were for losers who couldn't make it where the crowds gather and the fans cheer. While I can now see the error of my belief and immaturity, it was the way I saw it then. My father's encouragement did not make me feel any better, but I concluded that to play Church ball was better than not playing at all.

Bishop Shurtliff called Frank Palmer to coach. He knew the game better than the school coaches, but I didn't realize until years later that he understood boys were embryonic men waiting to discover themselves. He understood that careless shouting at a young player may change some immediate behavior but has the capacity to scar his image of himself and who he becomes both on and off the court. This wonderful man took less than a minute of his valuable time and planted a few seeds that have brought me a blessed harvest.

One day after we had practiced for about an hour, he closed the practice session, indicating it was time to get ready to go to mutual. He said the young women would like us better if we showered. He instructed us to go down to the men's showers in the basement of new stake center. Everyone, including Coach Palmer, vacated the gym and went to the shower room. I lingered, and all alone I shot for five or ten minutes in the large vacant gym. Then I saw Brother Palmer walk through the gym door and stop just inside. I could see him from the corner of my eye but pretended not to notice him. He was standing with his arms folded, watching me rather intently. I continued to shoot the basketball three or four times. He moved closer to me on the floor and said, "Hey Dave, would you repeat that jump shot you just did?" Nervously, I complied, thinking that I was a loser and an adult was about to criticize me and affirm why I had been cut from my high school team. In an effort to mimic the shot, I turned, set my feet, went straight up in the air, and shot the ball. I don't remember whether it went in the hoop or not. I do remember what Brother Palmer said to me though. "David, do you know who you remind me of when you shoot that jump shot? You look just like Melvin Daniels." (You may not know who Mel was, but I did. He was a great University of New Mexico player who went on to play with the NBA's Indiana Pacers). "You do! You look just like Melvin Daniels," he repeated. And then he added, "The way you turn, go straight up, and shoot, especially your wrist action, you look just like Mel Daniels." Then the bishop's emissary turned and walked away, leaving me alone again in the gym. I'm now pretty sure I wasn't alone. It was me, my ball, and my buddy Mel! How do you think I felt after Brother Palmer walked out? What shot do you think I practiced over and over? What new self-talk script do you think I accepted and uttered for the next twenty-five years? How do you think I saw myself when one of the significant adults in my life gave me permission to play like Mel? I now know that the validity of Brother Palmer's temple recommend was in jeopardy; he had just told one of the greatest lies ever uttered, especially inside of a dedicated church gymnasium. However, my mind grasped onto that idea, and in many ways it changed my life. How? Well, I didn't make it to the NBA, but I did make my high school team the next two years, enjoyed two great seasons, was selected to play in our state North-South all-star game, and received a scholarship to play college basketball.

Now, using the context of that experience, let me relate two practical things my parents did well to balance whatever they may have done alongside occasionally pointing out our faults, failings, and imperfections.

Dad's was couched in, "Hey David, let's go for a ride in the pickup truck!" I came to know what that meant and looked forward to it. Going for a ride in the truck meant he and I were going alone for a ride, which would span thirty minutes to an hour. He was a contractor and many times we would go check on the progress of two or three job sites. Other times we would just ride out into the canyons nearby or up on top of some bluffs overlooking our town. Once in a while we'd go do an errand at the bank or drop off a set of blueprints to a general contractor. One thing I knew was he'd have me captive to just talk as we rode. In my teen years things changed, and I knew that I'd have him captive.

Now, here's the catch to his genius as a parent. Sprinkled into our conversations were discussions about his business, with questions like, "David, you've got great insight. How do you think I should deal with this problem or that?" Or, "David, I've noticed that you're really good at developing ideas. What do you think about this idea?" Keep in mind that our conversations about his construction business started when I was a boy of eleven or twelve and continued into my young adult life. When I reflect on that, I say to myself, "Are you kidding? What good answer could come to an adult business problem from a twelve-year-old boy?" The answer is simple. Dad wasn't really looking for my insight as much as he was showing me that he loved me by expressing confidence in me. He was showing me he loved me by doing as Brother Palmer did: writing positive affirmations in my heart and mind, which made me feel valued. Come to think of it, like Frank Palmer, Dad certainly told a lie or two about how good I was at something. I loved those rides in the pickup, which came fairly often, because I felt loved, valued, appreciated, and blessed. Plus, it was a place where I also knew I could ask him questions (especially during those teen years). Dad's forum was the pickup truck.

For Mom, it was "bread day" at the kitchen table. Every Thursday, Mom made bread. Her hot bread with butter and honey was something to die for. As a boy, I'd have a slice or two and a glass of milk. As a teenager, I'd finish off one loaf and consume a quart of milk. I recall many times when it was just Mom and me sitting at the table. I don't remember if she ever joined me in eating the bread, but every time, she sat in the chair next to me and we talked. She would say, "David, ever since you were a little boy, I could see you have such potential." Or, "You are a hard worker." Or she would tell me a scripture story and then tell me how she saw those same positive virtues in me. With my mouth full, I was captive to allow her to voice loving positive affirmations while expressing her confidence in me to make good choices. On more than one occasion, I needed correction. It's amazing how hot bread and honey can soften and effectively inject chastisement into a boy. Her corrections usually came in the form of, "It's not like you to . . ." For example, "It's not like you to be disobedient. The real David I know is obedient." "David, it's not like you to be rude to your little sister. You are normally so kind to her. She considers you her hero." Or, "It's not like you to ever skip seminary." Those gentle "it's not like you" phrases were not attacking me, but rather they showed the way to becoming a better person.

These methods take time. It requires some investment and thought. Finding the right venue and the time to do it is taxing. I don't know where your venue will be. Maybe it's lying on the trampoline looking at the stars. Perhaps it will be after the drive thru at the local Dairy Queen, eating french fries or consuming a blizzard while you watch the sun set. Maybe it's walking or running together. Any forum or venue will work as long as it's captivating, positive, and time-appropriate. The rest will take care of itself.

Parenting Self-Examination

1. Do you communicate "I love you" in word as well as in expressing specifically how you value your child? How can you do better?
2. What's your venue or forum for expressing positive affirmations and showing how you value your child?
3. Consider your own life as a child. Can you find similar efforts by your parents to affirm your goodness? What will you want to do for your own children? Write these things in your journal.

Scriptures for Study

Ether 12:27	Genesis 1:26–27	Proverbs 3:26
2 Timothy 1:71	Corinthians 2:3–5	

A Parting Thought

Tell your children that you love them and that you are so happy to have them in your life. Recognize that Heavenly Father loves them too and remember that as parents we are His agents and must express our love and confidence in them. As you watch and pray for opportunities to show that you love them, remember that the Holy Ghost will be quick to help you know what, when, and how.

Remember: No recipes. Study. Self-examine. Do your best. Live worthy of the Holy Ghost. Pray that the Lord will touch your doings and consecrate them for the blessing and benefit of you, your children, and your grandchildren.

Principle 10

Tempers, Anger, and Voices

"Never forget that these little ones are the sons and daughters of God and that yours is a custodial relationship to them, that He was a parent before you were parents and that He has not relinquished His parental rights or interest in His little ones. Now, love them, take care of them. Fathers, control your tempers, now and in all the years to come. Mothers, control your voices; keep them down. Rear your children in love, in the nurture and admonition of the Lord. Take care of your little ones. Welcome them into your homes, and nurture and love them with all your hearts." (Gordon B Hinckley, Salt Lake University Third Stake conference, 3 November 1996)

I NOTICE THAT President Hinckley's counsel is based on the phrase "nurture and love them with all your hearts." President Hinckley also uses a phrase by Paul in Ephesians: "Provoke not your children to wrath: but bring them up in the nurture and admonition of the Lord" ("The Environment of Our Homes," *Ensign*, June 1985; Ephesians 6:4). The common word used is *nurture*.

That's an interesting word—*nurture*. It's a derivative of Middle English and Old French that means "nourishment," "to feed," or "to cherish." The dictionary thesaurus gives the following words as synonymous terms to describe *nurture*: *bring up, care for, cultivate, support, encourage, develop, boost, contribute to, assist, strengthen, fortify*. Sometimes in understanding a word, it's helpful to know what it doesn't mean. An antonym for *nurture* is *hinder*.

It sounds like our role is to cherish children and seek to give them a boost. After all, they are God's children and on loan to us. We are in a real sense custodians or stewards of His children, given to us to care for, bring up, cultivate, support, encourage, develop, and boost. Our charge is to contribute to their lives and assist, strengthen, and fortify them.

Both President Hinckley and Paul suggest that wrath, anger, tempers, and raised voices hinder this process. The reason is obvious: contention, with flaring tempers and yelling voices, drives the Spirit away, and we are left on our own to bring up His children. With the Spirit's help and guidance, we have a chance of guiding and lifting them. We are not the teachers. That's the role of the real teacher, the Holy Ghost. Chase Him out of the equation and we become raspy, unpleasant, and preachy voices, which invite either quiet, angry submission or like responses in screaming tones. I have learned in my own case that the tone of voice is as important to control as the raised or loud voice. Cynicism and sarcastic tones are just as effective in chasing the Spirit away as a raised voices and violent tempers.

"Get out of my room!" shouts a teenager at a younger sibling.

"I hate you! You always take my things," one small child says to another.

"You make me so mad when you do that! What a stupid thing to do!" yells one family member to another.

With eyes rolling and a mumbling tone, a father says to an eleven-year-old son, "You don't get it, do you? You are working your way to being grounded for the next five years. You are a piece of work!"

These expressions of anger happen all the time in some families. Contention and discord may be a natural tendency when a group of people share the same space in a home. The Church provides this counsel:

> It is true that there is a rare time and place for the expression of righteous anger—the Lord himself has expressed indignation and anger when the circumstances warranted such reactions. Righteous anger is a controlled response to an unrighteous situation, however, not the kind of emotional outbursts most of us are all too familiar with. It is this uncontrolled, emotion-charged anger—and the attendant contention that arises out of it—that is referred to in this article.
>
> Irritations and frustrations will occur in our homes, but frequent anger and contention do not persist where the gospel of Jesus Christ is practiced. A unified effort by both children and parents can bring into the home a spirit of love that can defuse anger and establish peace, respect, and trust.
>
> In many ways, expressions of unrighteous anger have their roots in selfishness. Those who respond with anger when they are frustrated or annoyed are saying, in effect, that their feelings and opinions are more important than those of others. If circumstances or the actions of others do not coincide with what they think should be, such individuals are offended and become angry.
>
> In the same way, selfish people sometimes use anger as a way to control others. With many, it is the preferred means

of manipulating people, especially their children. By raising their voices and acting mad, they make others give in to them. Unfortunately, as parents use this tactic with their children, the children adopt anger as the way to respond to anything they cannot control. A pattern of anger is established and passed from parents to children generation after generation until, somehow, the cycle is broken.

The key to overcoming a spirit of anger and contention, then, is to overcome selfishness—to try to infuse empathy and compassion into our relationships. ("Dealing with Anger and Contention," *Ensign*, September 1988)

One of my favorite people shared with me her experience. By her own admission, she grew up in a family that just tended to be loud. They talked loud, played loud, interacted loud, and even sang loud in Church meetings. As a result, this carried over to her parenting. When her kids acted up, they were loud and she reacted to them in loud tones. One day a friend shared an article with her that gave some insight and counsel about raised voices. She determined that it was time to break the cycle. Her determination to speak in softer tones and not react in an elevated voice bore immediate fruit. Her softer voice invited softer responses.

President Wilford Woodruff gave this counsel: "I made up my mind years ago to be governed by certain principles. I resolved that I would never be controlled by my passions . . . nor by anger, but that I would govern myself. This resolution I have endeavored to carry out in my life" (Matthias Cowley, *Wilford Woodruff* [Salt Lake City: Bookcraft, 1964], 397).

Perhaps the best resolve is to decide and commit not to be ruled by anger or raised voices. However, we can be sure that those around us will seldom have a matched resolution and will undoubtedly test us.

The same *Ensign* article mentioned earlier provides some excellent counsel:

The gospel of Jesus Christ offers the only enduring solution to the problems of contention. Even so, parents often need some temporary solutions to quarreling or fighting. But the spiritual illness only becomes more difficult to cure when busy parents fail to follow this short-term care with the more thorough treatment of charity that the gospel of Jesus Christ provides. First-aid for anger may include the following:

1. Avoid reacting with anger when a child explodes in a tantrum. But if you do become angry, let your feelings subside before disciplining the child. Do something to let off steam, like taking a walk around the block or putting the offender in a designated "timeout place" until you cool down.

2. If your child is angry, decline to give in to his angry demands until he finds a better way to handle his emotions.

3. Ignore a child's outburst, but not his feelings. Acknowledging a child's feelings assures him that you care and allows him to see you as part of his recovery rather than as his enemy.

4. If children are very young, try distracting them. Distraction may help the child forget his anger and give you time to deal with the root of the problem at a better time.

To permanently rid ourselves and our families of anger and the spirit of contention we must develop a spirit of unselfishness. Such a spirit attends sincere effort to think of others before ourselves and to cultivate the gift of charity ("Dealing with Anger and Contention," *Ensign*, September 1988).

Parenting Self-Examination

1. Determining where you currently are provides a basis for finding ways to improve. On a scale of 1 to 10, with 10 being a complete contention-free environment and 1 being a chronic case of fighting, where would you rate your home? Now decide two things you can do personally to improve by just one number in the next week.

2. Have a family council or family home evening and discuss ways to decrease selfishness.

3. Privately ask your spouse and a child to help you with your resolve. Invite them to do the same. Help each other.

Scriptures for Study

Proverbs 29:11   Proverbs 15:1, 18   James 1:19–20
Colossians 3:8   Nephi 11:29–30   Alma 38:12

A Parting Thought

It's not likely that we will fix our contention issues all at once. Regardless of where you feel you are currently, be grateful for incremental steps and improvement. When you personally do better with controlling your temper, your voice, or cynicism, quietly celebrate your progress. When those around you do a little better, make a big deal about it with them and say thanks. Comment about how you are feeling much better about the progress. When someone slips, don't make a big deal out of it. Remind them that it's okay and to try again.

> Remember: No recipes. Study. Self-examine. Do your best. Live worthy of the Holy Ghost. Pray that the Lord will touch your doings and consecrate them for the blessing and benefit of you, your children, and your grandchildren.

Principle 11

Women—A Secret Weapon

"As daughters of our Heavenly Father, and as daughters of Eve, we are all mothers and we have always been mothers. And we each have the responsibility to love and help lead the rising generation. . . . As mothers in Israel, we are the Lord's secret weapon. Our influence comes from a divine endowment that has been in place from the beginning. [In the premortal world, when our Father described our role, I wonder if we didn't stand in wide-eyed wonder that He would bless us with a sacred trust so central to His plan and that He would endow us with gifts so vital to the loving and leading of His children.] I wonder if we shouted for joy at least in part because of the ennobling stature He gave us in His kingdom. The world won't tell you that, but the Spirit will. (Sheri L. Dew, "Are We Not All Mothers?" *Ensign*, November 2001)

I HAVE BEEN impressed with two wonderful women in the Book of Mormon whose courageous acts impacted multitudes, even millions, over time. One was only a brief headliner on one dramatic occasion, and the other one's name was never disclosed.

Abish was a Lamanite woman who looked on as an observer in the sensational conversion process of King Lamoni, his wife, and his servants. This spiritual evolution began when King Lamoni was overpowered by the Spirit to the extent that to his wife he appeared to be dead. Ammon, a new missionary among the Lamanites, consoled the queen by informing her, "He is not dead, but he sleepeth in God, and on the morrow he shall rise again" (Alma 19:8). As indicated by Ammon, King Lamoni did rise on the following day and declared that he had seen the Savior. It was a moving and spiritual moment as he told his wife, the queen, about his experience. Then he sunk to the earth again, being overpowered by the Spirit. This time his wife sunk also. Ammon began to express his gratitude and love in prayer to God, and he too was overcome by the Spirit and sunk to the ground. The kings servants soon followed, being overcome by that same power, and fell to the earth—all except Abish. Years earlier, she was converted by an experience of her father when he had received a remarkable vision. She had never disclosed her testimony, but she understood the workings of the Spirit well enough that she thought this was an opportunity to share her light and knowledge with others. Leaving

Ammon and the king, queen, and servants lying on the ground under the influence of the Spirit, she went and joyfully informed the people. However, as a large group assembled, they did not see it as she did. They saw a light-skinned Nephite and the king, queen, and servants prostrate and assumed that Ammon was a monster or one who had come to afflict them. In a scene of dispute and sharp contention,

> [Abish] went and took the queen by the hand, that perhaps she might raise her from the ground; and as soon as she touched her hand she arose and stood upon her feet, and cried with a loud voice, saying: O blessed Jesus, who has saved me from an awful hell! O blessed God, have mercy on this people!
>
> And when she had said this, she clasped her hands, being filled with joy, speaking many words which were not understood; and when she had done this, she took the king, Lamoni, by the hand, and behold he arose and stood upon his feet.
>
> And he, immediately, seeing the contention among his people, went forth and began to rebuke them, and to teach them the words which he had heard from the mouth of Ammon; and as many as heard his words believed, and were converted unto the Lord.
>
> But there were many among them who would not hear his words; therefore they went their way.
>
> And it came to pass that when Ammon arose he also administered unto them, and also did all the servants of Lamoni; and they did all declare unto the people the selfsame thing—that their hearts had been changed; that they had no more desire to do evil. (Alma 19:29–33)

That critical event was the first small wave in what became a tsunami of quality conversions among the Lamanites, which completely altered Book of Mormon history.

Abish's courage, trust in God, and quiet testimony were pivotal. She was a "secret weapon" for assisting the Lord in lifting an entire nation. Her seemingly insignificant role in this story of change leads us, a few years later, to the inspiring accounts of the missionary success of the four sons of Mosiah, the Anti-Nephi-Lehies burying their weapons as a symbol of their change, the 2,060 stripling warriors, and Samuel the Lamanite, to name a few.

Earlier in the Book of Mormon, a nameless young woman took courage in an unpopular moment and created a wave of change that saved the life of Nephi. In this story, Laman, Lemuel, and those in Ishmael's family who hated Nephi sought to kill him. Nephi petitioned the Lord to give him strength to break away, and when the bands broke, his murderous brothers and friends redoubled the efforts of their assault and bound him again.

Watch the dynamics of what happened next:

> And it came to pass that they were angry with me again, and sought to lay hands upon me; but behold, one of the daughters of Ishmael, yea, and also her mother, and one of the sons of Ishmael, did plead with my brethren, insomuch that they did soften their hearts; and they did cease striving to take away my life. . . .
>
> They were sorrowful, because of their wickedness, insomuch that they did bow down before me, and did plead with me that I would forgive them of the thing that they had done against me.
>
> And it came to pass that I did frankly forgive them all that they had done. (1 Nephi 7:19–21)

Did you notice that one of the daughters of Ishmael started the ripple and was then joined by Ishmael's wife and son? The power of one young woman created an environment where others joined her in exerting influence that resulted in changing hearts and saving Nephi's life.

One parent taking courage to stand in unpopular moments, sometimes even in small and insignificant things, can impact many lives. It's not easy to say no to a begging child. It's difficult to take a courageous stand and teach standards from the *For the Strength of Youth* pamphlet to a struggling teenager with love.

I see the Lord's "secret weapons" all around me: nurturing neighbors and families reaching out to those in need, a Relief Society president giving endless service, young mothers sharing inspiring messages in sacrament meeting whose lives testify of their love and dedication to their children and the Lord. I see single mothers who keep the family glued together and stable in turbulent times. I'm inspired by unmarried, childless angels who remember the birthday of every member of the ward and affirm the goodness they see in others everywhere they go. Yes, I see the Lord's secret weapons and am in awe.

Sister Dew asks,

> How will our young women learn to live as women of God unless they see what women of God look like, meaning what we wear, watch, and read; how we fill our time and our minds; how we face temptation and uncertainty; where we find true joy; and why modesty and femininity are hallmarks of righteous women? How will our young men learn to value women of God if we don't show them the virtue of our virtues? . . .
>
> Look around. Who needs you and your influence? <u>If we really want to make a difference</u>, it will happen as we mother those we have borne and those we are willing to bear with. If we will stay right with our [children]—meaning, if we will love them—in most cases they will stay right with us—meaning, they will let us lead them." ("Are We Not All Mothers?" *Ensign*, November 2001)

Parenting Self-Examination

1. Sister Dew asks, "Who needs you and your influence?" Which of your own children needs a little extra help? <u>Which of their friends need to see your courage and the power of your example and testimony</u>?
2. Is there anything you've been "waffling" (being wishy-washy)

on lately that you know in your heart needs your courage to improve?

3. Take a few minutes and write in your journal about ways you can be a "secret weapon" in the Lord's arsenal. How can you be a stronger father or mother and better example to your children? How can you be the one father or mother who leads your children and their friends in daily matters of kindness, love, charity, and other Christlike attributes?

Scriptures for Study

Alma 19:29–33	1 Nephi 7:19–21	Alma 19:16–36
Joshua 23:10–11	Philippians 2:13	

A Parting Thought

Courage is defined with words like *spunk*, *gallantry*, and *fearlessness*. The valor and grit of courage must rely on a foundation of knowing what we are fighting for. I have a testimony that we can be sure Heavenly Father loves us and our children. He also loves our children's friends and other parents who need a little boost and support from us in providing examples. Take heart and know that there is power in one. You be the one. Inspire your children with courage to also be the one in their circles. Heavenly Father is interested.

Remember: No recipes. Study. Self-examine. Do your best. Live worthy of the Holy Ghost. Pray that the Lord will touch your doings and consecrate them for the blessing and benefit of you, your children, and your grandchildren.

* You and God are a majority

Principle 12

Conspicuous Living

"Parents simply cannot flirt with skepticism or cynicism, then be surprised when their children expand that flirtation into full-blown romance. If in matters of faith and belief children are at risk of being swept downstream by this intellectual current or that cultural rapid, we as their parents must be more certain than ever to hold to anchored, unmistakable moorings clearly recognizable to those of our own household. It won't help anyone if we go over the edge with them, explaining through the roar of the falls all the way down that we really did know the Church was true and that the keys of the priesthood really were lodged there but we just didn't want to stifle anyone's freedom to think otherwise. No, we can hardly expect the children to get to shore safely if the parents don't seem to know where to anchor their own boat. . . . Brothers and sisters, our children take their flight into the future with our thrust and with our aim." (Jeffrey R. Holland, "A Prayer for the Children," *Ensign*, May 2003)

MY GRANDFATHER Christensen used to tell us stories about his father, my great-grandfather Otto Edward William Thorwald Christensen, who as a young boy (age ten) joined the Church with his mother and brothers in Denmark in the year 1850. Four principle names surface in records and journals: Apostle Erastus Snow, Peter O. Hansen, George Parker Dykes, and John Erik Forsgren. There were others who accompanied them as well. As Grandpa spoke of our family roots and the blessings of the gospel in our lives, he always spoke with reverence and gratitude of those missionaries who accepted the call to travel to Scandinavia to share the message of the Restoration.

There was one name that Grandpa always included—John Erik Forsgren. At the conclusion of his mission, John Erik Forsgren was asked to take a company of Danish converts from Denmark across the sea and plains to the Salt Lake Valley. The new Christensen converts could not all make the exodus for lack of funds. It was determined that twelve-year-old Otto William Edward Thorwald would go with John Erik Forsgren alone, leaving his mother and brothers to come at a later date. In sharing this story, each generation has thought about the difficulty of that choice and has been grateful. Suffice it to say, John Erik Forsgren became a name our family reverenced and appreciated at hero status.

There is more of Brother Forsgren's story Grandpa didn't tell. After years of dedicated service to the Church and the kingdom of God, John got offended. The record is silent as to why, but researchers indicate it likely started over a piece of land he felt entitled to, or perhaps because he didn't receive a calling in the Church he felt he deserved. He slid down the slippery slope of apostasy and was finally excommunicated. Later he openly denounced Brigham Young and professed to be the real prophet. The years that followed were not good. An eccentric, he set up a tent on the east bench of the Salt Lake Valley and became know as the "Bench Prophet," speaking out against Brigham Young and other Church leaders, including his old missionary companion Erastus Snow. It has been said by Forsgren family descendants that after decades of service and testimony in the restored Church, in consequence of John's apostasy and negative example, Brigham Young stated that John's descendents would lose out on the blessings of the gospel into the third and fourth generations.

And it has been so! John's descendents—particularly the men—have largely remained bitter and estranged from the Church. Often the men would marry a good woman who would ensure that the children or grandchildren were baptized and occasionally received the Aaronic Priesthood, but the line has remained distant from Church activity and has been without important blessings.

Tragically, this once-wonderful missionary and example of sacrifice and service in the kingdom of God, who to this day is celebrated in Scandinavian Church history in the annual pageant as

Gavle Sweden—a hero—fell away and took many of his descendants with him. He had been like a father to my great-grandfather Otto Edward William Thorwald.

Our actions, decisions, lifestyles, and testimonies as parents are critical. Anyone who says that what they do and how they live this life is their business and won't affect anyone but them is derelict. Of course a parent's choices and attitudes impact the generations that follow. The quote by Elder Holland continues:

> Not long ago Sister Holland and I met a fine young man who came in contact with us after he had been roaming around through the occult and sorting through a variety of Eastern religions, all in an attempt to find religious faith. His father, he admitted, believed in nothing whatsoever. But his grandfather, he said, was actually a member of The Church of Jesus Christ of Latter-day Saints. "But he didn't do much with it," the young man said. "He was always pretty cynical about the Church." From a grandfather who is cynical to a son who is agnostic to a grandson who is now looking desperately for what God had already once given his family! (Ibid.)

My heart aches for the descendents of John Erik Forsgren. He went from a hero missionary and emigrant company leader who loved and inspired hundreds of new converts to a quirky "Bench Prophet" who passed on to his own posterity bitterness, bad attitude, and a lifestyle that has not included any of the blessings of which he taught and testified. I spoke personally to one of the descendents of John Erik who told me that if it were not for his grandmother, he wouldn't have been baptized. If it were not for his grandmother, he wouldn't have been ordained a deacon. He said, "I didn't understand why, but many of my family—uncles, cousins, and father—only talked about the Church in a tone of distance, ill feelings, or even bitterness. We never said prayers or had scriptures or went to Church. It's just the way it's been all my life."

Note: I will pause this tragic story until the next chapter. There is an ending you won't want to miss.

What we do, how we say it, and the feelings we demonstrate will get passed on. How we talk about the bishop, ward, and stake leaders matters. Our Church attendance and participation is important. Whether or not prayer is a part of our home and personal life will be perpetuated on to our children and grandchildren. How we feel and talk about tithing, the Word of Wisdom, and general conference will, in large measure, be part of the inheritance we give the next generations. It all matters!

Elder Richard L. Evans taught this important principle:

> Sometimes some parents mistakenly feel that they can relax a little as to conduct and conformity or take perhaps a so called liberal view of basic and fundamental things—thinking that a little laxness or indulgence won't matter—or they may fail to teach or to attend Church, or may voice critical views. Some parents . . . seem to feel that they can ease up a little on the fundamentals without affecting their family or their family's future. But if a parent goes a little off course, the children are likely to exceed the parent's example. (In Conference Report, October 1964, 135–36)

I believe the opposite is also true. My grandparents were awesome and passed on a legacy of faith. I can see that my parents were a little better than my grandparents in a lot of ways. In observing my parents' children, it seems we have likewise stepped it up a notch and have done even better. I marvel as I watch my own children and how they've taken the teachings we struggled to pass on to them, and they're doing better than we ever did. I am counting on my grandchildren to live at a higher spiritual level and my great-grandchildren to take it higher yet. It is a pattern worth paying attention to. As Elder Evans states, "the children are likely to exceed the parent's example" either positively or negatively. We have a great responsibility.

Parenting Self-Examination

1. Are you carrying or unconsciously exhibiting any attitudes or voicing any indulgences that have the potential of misdirecting your children? How do you support leaders?

2. Go to the Lord in prayer and ask that He help you to know if there's anything you are displaying to your children or grand-children that might be misinterpreted or misunderstood as "off course." The Lord is interested, and the Holy Ghost will help you to know.

3. What positive attitudes and traits do you desire to pass on to the next generation? Take out a piece of paper and write them down. What are you doing and how can you improve to make sure they internalize and live them?

4. Write your testimony in your journal for future generations to know precisely how you feel about the gospel.

Scriptures for Study

| Enos 1:1, 3 | Proverbs 22:6 | 1 Nephi 1:1 |
| Moroni 7:1 | 2 Nephi 4:3–7 | |

A Parting Thought

I love how Elder Holland challenges us to "live the gospel as conspicuously as you can. Keep the covenants your children know you have made. Give priesthood blessings. And bear your testimony! Don't just assume your children will somehow get the drift of your beliefs on their own" ("A Prayer for the Children," *Ensign*, May 2003). May I echo that same challenge to be conspicuous in the way we live the gospel—not self-righteous or the least bit pharisaic, but rather quiet, good examples of all that matters. It is my testimony that as we do, our children will take their aim and flight to heavenly heights. May we all be conspicuous in the way we live the gospel.

Remember: No recipes. Study. Self-examine. Do your best. Live worthy of the Holy Ghost. Pray that the Lord will touch your doings and consecrate them for the blessing and benefit of you, your children, and your grandchildren.

Principle 13

Remember the Rescue

"The Prophet Joseph Smith declared—and he never taught more comforting doctrine—that the eternal sealings of faithful parents and the divine promises made to them for valiant service in the Cause of Truth, would save not only themselves, but likewise their posterity. Though some of the sheep may wander, the eye of the Shepherd is upon them, and sooner or later they will feel the tentacles of Divine Providence reaching out after them and drawing them back to the fold. Either in this life or the life to come, they will return. They will have to pay their debt to justice; they will suffer for their sins; and may tread a thorny path; but if it leads them at last, like the penitent Prodigal, to a loving and forgiving father's heart and home, the painful experience will not have been in vain. Pray for your careless and disobedient children; hold on to them with your faith. Hope on, trust on, till you see the salvation of God." (Orson F. Whitney, in Conference Report, April 1929, 110)

YOU LIKELY know parents who have done everything right and yet are puzzled why one or more of their children lose their way. They worry and feel helpless, sometimes used and abused. I have known several of these great Saints—parents who have applied the teachings and principles of the gospel, yet still a child strays.

Elder Boyd K. Packer taught:

It is a great challenge to raise a family in the darkening mists of our moral environment.

We emphasize that the greatest work you will do will be within the walls of your home, and that "no other success can compensate for failure in the home."

The measure of our success as parents, however, will not rest solely on how our children turn out. That judgment would be just only if we could raise our families in a perfectly moral environment, and that now is not possible.

It is not uncommon for responsible parents to lose one of their children, for a time, to influences over which they have no control. They agonize over rebellious sons or daughters. They are puzzled over why they are so helpless when they have tried so hard to do what they should.

It is my conviction that those wicked influences one day will be overruled. . . .

We cannot overemphasize the value of temple marriage, the binding ties of the sealing ordinance, and the standards of worthiness required of them. When parents keep the covenants they have made at the altar of the temple, their children will be forever bound to them. ("Our Moral Environment," *Ensign*, May 1992)

President Brigham Young said:

Let the father and mother, who are members of this Church and Kingdom, take a righteous course, and strive with all their might never to do a wrong, but to do good all their lives; if they have one child or one hundred children, if they conduct themselves towards them as they should, binding them to the Lord by their faith and prayers, I care not where those children go, they are bound up to their parents by an everlasting tie, and no power of earth or hell can separate them from their parents in eternity; they will return again to the fountain from whence they sprang. (*Teaching of Presidents of the Church: Brigham*

Young [Salt Lake City: The Church of Jesus Christ of Latter-day Saints, 1997], 163–69)

It is difficult to watch a child in self-destruct mode. I have a testimony that the Lord is mindful of our efforts as parents and is also lovingly mindful our children—they are His too!

President James E. Faust taught, "To those brokenhearted parents who have been righteous, diligent, and prayerful in the teaching of their disobedient children, we say to you, the Good Shepherd is watching over them" ("Dear Are the Sheep That Have Wandered," *Ensign*, May 2003). I believe that. Orson F. Whitney stated that they must suffer and pay their debt to justice. However, in this life or the life to come, they will return. Our covenants will be like a safety net that provides ways and means to save our families.

Elder Richard G. Scott reminded the parents in the Church,

When you have done all that you can reasonably do, rest the burden in the hands of the Lord.

When I take a small pebble and place it directly in front of my eye, it takes on the appearance of a mighty boulder. It is all I can see. It becomes all-consuming—like the problems of a loved one that affect our lives every waking moment. When the things you realistically can do to help are done, leave the matter in the hands of the Lord and worry no more. Do not feel guilty because you cannot do more. Do not waste your energy on useless worry. The Lord will take the pebble that fills your vision and cast it down among the challenges you will face in your eternal progress. It will then be seen in perspective. In time, you will feel impressions and know how to give further help. You will find more peace and happiness, will not neglect others that need you, and will be able to give greater help because of that eternal perspective. ("To Help a Loved One in Need," *Ensign*, May 1988)

While the teachings of Elders Whitney, Packer, and Scott and

Presidents Young and McKay give hope and promise to faithful parents, it is important to understand and remember that agency and accountability are fundamental to true doctrine. Hence, so are consequences. The Lord is clear that "men will be punished for their own sins, and not for Adam's transgression" (Articles of Faith 1:2). It follows that the only one who atones for the sins of another is our Lord and Savior, Jesus Christ. In other words, all who transgress the Lord's commandments or break their covenants must either repent or suffer for their own sins. Choices, either positive or negative, can impact others, but ultimately we all choose and receive the consequences of our own choices. However, the promises to parents who make and keep their covenants, repent, and endure to the end can have an important influence on wayward children. In his helpful *Ensign* article, Elder David A. Bednar teaches,

> The 'tentacles of Divine Providence' described by Elder Whitney may be considered a type of spiritual power, a heavenly pull or tug that entices a wandering child to return to the fold eventually. Such an influence cannot override the moral agency of a child but nonetheless can invite and beckon. Ultimately, a child must exercise his or her moral agency and respond in faith, repent with full purpose of heart, and act in accordance with the teachings of Christ. ("Faithful Parents and Wayward Children: Sustaining Hope While Overcoming Misunderstanding," *Ensign*, March 2014)

Perhaps there is divine assistance from both sides of the veil that is a consequence of righteous parents seeking to rescue sidetracked children. My son, Aaron, and his wife, Michelle, moved to Logan, Utah, a few years back. They reached out to and became friends with neighbors Jake and Jana. They were good people who attended Church on occasion, but they had reservations about serving and making covenants. They were a wonderful couple who had recently adopted a one-year-old daughter.

Over the next couple of years, my son's friendship with them grew stronger, and eventually their neighborly visits became more focused on the spiritual aspects of life. Jake's parents were not active members of the Church, but his grandmother was. She made sure that when he turned eight he was baptized. He didn't return again until he turned twelve, when he attended a few times and was ordained a deacon. Jake had lots of questions and concerns about doctrines like tithing and polygamy. He wondered why most of his paternal family were members but never talked about the Church unless it was in tones of cynicism or bitterness. As neighborly discussions and relationship turned more to gospel-related subjects, Jake and Jana began to attend Church meetings regularly. A spark of faith ignited in their souls, and in time they became fully active and made preparations to go to the temple to be sealed as a family.

Now "rescued" members, both Jake and Jana became particularly interested in deceased ancestors and desired to do all they could to let the impact of their faith make a difference, especially for Jake's family, who seemed to have had one foot in the Church. In that process, the Spirit of Elijah awakened a desire in them to learn more about their pasts.

On one particular visit to the Family History Library in Salt Lake City, they were having a hard time finding relevant information. Someone suggested they go to the Scandinavian section of the library and ask the couple missionaries there for help. They went upstairs, found a missionary, and asked if perhaps he could help them find Jake's great-great-great-grandfather. The missionary, who was to complete his mission days later, asked, "So what is the name of your great-great-great-grandfather?" Jake answered, "John Erik Forsgren." "Yes, I think I can help," replied the missionary as tears began to well up in his eyes. He then told the story of the first Swedish convert who had immigrated to America and was baptized in Boston. He spoke of this great man who had given his heart and soul to the Church, preached the gospel with power and authority, became a member of the Mormon Battalion, and then was called to serve a mission with Apostle Erastus Snow to Denmark and Sweden. Jake and Jana learned that John Erik Forsgren had been an extraordinary missionary with much success. He found his brother Peter who was ill, gave him a priesthood blessing that resulted in a miracle of healing, and converted and baptized him. They learned that John had led a company of Danish and Swedish converts from their homelands to Zion. They learned of his love for the people of the pioneer company, inspiring them daily with his testimony and faith in the living God. They were stunned, pleased, and surprised to know of Jake's deep roots to the Restoration.

They then learned the rest of the story. It unfolded that after a time, John had been offended, disaffected, and was ultimately excommunicated from the Church. He became an eccentric, bitter man professing to be a prophet. In fact, he was called the "Bench Prophet" who resided in a tent on the east bench in Salt Lake City. Then they learned that Brigham Young had made a statement to Jake's great-great-great-grandfather that in consequence of his attitude and bitterness, his posterity would be kept from the blessings of the restored gospel into the third and fourth generations. Imagine the feelings in Jake's and Jana's hearts.

As Jake and Jana shared the story with their friends, Aaron and Michelle, a familiar family name of heroic status surfaced: John Erik Forsgren, the revered surrogate father of twelve-year-old Otto William Edward Thorwald Christensen, who was in the company John led from Scandinavia to Germany to Liverpool and finally across the plains to the Salt Lake Valley. An interesting orchestration of events. The great-great-grandson of that twelve-year-old boy, Otto Edward William Thorwald Christensen, moved next door to the great-great-great-grandson of John Erik Forsgren in the third and fourth generation. A sweet rescue of Jake and Jana occurred, and they in turn have been saviors to hundreds of family members of those floundering generations. I can tell you that there were tears of joy and gratitude as Jake and Aaron shared their common history—one thanking the other for the gospel brought to Scandinavia and the other for his help with the rescue, which occurred precisely as prophesied.

Let's make and keep covenants. Let's do the best we can do. Allow the Lord in His omniscience to orchestrate and care for His children.

Parenting Self-Examination

1. How can you show your trust and confidence in the Lord's promises about watching and caring for your children?
2. Do you know any parents who need to be reminded of the promises of the Lord regarding wayward children? Take steps to share your testimony of those promises.
3. Take an opportunity to write in your journal your feelings about the gospel, missionary stories in your family, the rescue of wandering souls, and your role in them.

Scriptures for Study

3 Nephi 21:1–17   Abraham 1:1–18   Luke 15:11–32

Title page of the Book of Mormon, second paragraph: "That they may know the covenants of the Lord, that they are not cast off forever."

A Parting Thought

I'd like to use the words of President James E. Faust to conclude this chapter:

> It is very unfair and unkind to judge conscientious and faithful parents because some of their children rebel or stray from the teachings and love of their parents. . . . We should be considerate of those worthy, righteous parents who struggle and suffer with disobedient children. One of my friends used to say, "If you have never had any problems with your children, just wait

awhile." . . . When parents mourn for disobedient and way-ward children we must, with compassion, "forbid the casting of the first stone. ("Dear Are the Sheep That Have Wandered," *Ensign*, May 2003)

> Remember: No recipes. Study. Self-examine. Do your best. Live worthy of the Holy Ghost. Pray that the Lord will touch your doings and consecrate them for the blessing and benefit of you, your children, and your grandchildren.

Principle 14

The Power of Presiding

"My father died when I was seven. I was the oldest of three small children our widowed mother struggled to raise. When I was ordained a deacon, she said how pleased she was to have a priesthood holder in the home. But Mother continued to direct the family, including call-ing on which one of us would pray when we knelt together each morn-ing. I was puzzled. I had been taught that the priesthood presided in the family. There must be something I didn't know about how that principle worked. . . . When my father died, my mother presided over our family. She had no priesthood office, but as the surviving parent in her marriage she had become the governing officer in her family. At the same time, she was always totally respectful of the priesthood authority of our bishop and other Church leaders. She presided over her family, but they presided over the Church. . . . The faithful wid-owed mother who raised us had no confusion about the eternal nature of the family. (Dallin H. Oaks, "Priesthood Authority in the Family and the Church," *Ensign*, November 2005)

M Y MOTHER was an angel, and her three sisters are just like her. I am in possession of a photograph of those four sisters together, standing with their husbands, who were all ordained patriarchs in the Church. The four patriarchs, my mother, and one of her sisters have all since passed to the other side of the veil. These four good and righteous women and their faithful husbands are the parents of twenty children and have scores of grandchildren and a multitude of great- and even great-great grandchildren. If you were able to look into the faces of these women, you would see a common kindness, charity, and godliness in each. However, I think it's important to understand that these spiritual pillars where shaped and honed, becoming great over the years. Yes, each were tested and tried by the furnace of adversity.

Aunts Ethelyn and Lavern each experienced the challenge of going through ugly and heart-breaking divorces. Details are not important here, but circumstances and broken covenants are familiar with many today. In short, they were dealt a circumstance that required they raise their families without a strong companion. Through it all, they remained true and faithful, and the Lord blessed them with righteous companions after their children had created homes of their own.

During my boyhood and teenage days, I was a quiet observer to it all. In the case of Aunt Laverne, it was a little more up close and personal since we resided in the same town. While I knew that my dad and my uncles were mindful of Laverne, I never saw her as being a single mother. She was "the mother" to her kids, and I knew and loved her as a very special aunt. She and her children lived life the same as the rest of the families. They attended extended family functions together just like the other uncles, aunts, and cousins in the grand family circle. I never wondered, and to this day I assume that Laverne presided in the home. When we visited her home, she was the one who called on one of us to bless the food or offer the family prayer. She was the one who was in charge. If she or one of her children needed a priesthood blessing, she was the one who called upon priesthood holders to do it.

The word *preside* is defined as being in a position of authority or to be in charge. The word is synonymous with "responsible," "administer," "to be the head of," "direct," "command," "lead," "oversee," and "govern."

Elder Oaks shares this little personal experience:

> I recall an experience that shows the effect of [my mother's] teachings. Just before Christmas one year, our bishop asked me, as a deacon, to help him deliver Christmas baskets to the widows of the ward. I carried a basket to each door with his greetings. When he drove me home, there was one basket remaining. He handed it to me and said it was for my mother. As he drove away, I stood in the falling snow wondering why there was a basket for my mother. She never referred to herself as a widow, and it had never occurred to me that she was. To a 12-year-old boy, she wasn't a widow. She had a husband, and we had a father. He was just away for a while. (Ibid.)

To single mothers, understand that you preside in your home. You're the one who has the authority to be in charge. You are the one who administers and directs. You are the governess of the household. With the overseer role comes the responsibility to lead in the Lord's way. Most two-parent households will have occasions when the husband will be away on business or will serve in Church callings that require him to be out of the home. While he is gone, you preside. You must lead in matters of discipline without needing to say, "Just wait until Dad gets home." Fathers must support and sustain their spouses, who preside when they are gone. That means standing behind the decisions they are required to make when fathers are not available.

Traditional couples and single parents take notice: There is great blessing and strength that rests in the hearts and minds of children when they feel and understand that in whatever circumstance there is someone who presides. There is confusion and potential testing when they don't have that peace of mind.

Parenting Self-Examination

1. Did anything come to your mind as you read this chapter that nudged you to change or tweak a practice in your home? Act upon it.
2. Do you know anyone who might benefit from Elder Oak's instruction? Share it.
3. Consider your experience with the subject. Are there positive examples that demonstrate the key points and doctrines considered in this chapter? Crystallize your experiences by writing in your personal journal. Some future reader may be blessed by it.

Scriptures for Study

D&C 121:37   D&C 121:41–43
D&C 121:45–46

A Parting Thought

It has been my blessing to know and be inspired by wonderful people who have had to raise families in single-parent homes. Their level of discipleship is awe-inspiring. Their charitable hearts and sweet dispositions are great examples to me. I am thinking of a person I know who lost her husband in a tragic accident, leaving her with four children to raise. Her faithful and consecrated life was evident to her bishop when she brought a check and a donation slip to him in his office one Sunday afternoon. She indicated she knew it was unusual to give fast offerings in this way, but she asked if it could be treated with a special confidentiality. When she handed the slip and check to the bishop, he noted that it was a large amount of money. "Sister, you don't need to do this," the bishop said to her. She had received a large sum of insurance proceeds and felt that the amount she was giving was surplus. "You don't need to do this," the bishop repeated. This sister looked into the eyes of the bishop and explained, "The Lord has been so very good to me. I have been blessed with the ability to provide for my family, their education, and their future and mine. I have no debt, and I have a savings nest egg. I have paid my tithing and this is excess." Then she repeated, "The Lord has been so good to me—this is His." Faithful living brings extraordinary blessings and blesses many others.

Remember: No recipes. Study. Self-examine. Do your best. Live worthy of the Holy Ghost. Pray that the Lord will touch your doings and consecrate them for the blessing and benefit of you, your children, and your grandchildren.

Principle 15

Christ-Centered Parenting

"We hold in our arms the rising generation. They come to this earth with important responsibilities and great spiritual capacities. We cannot be casual in how we prepare them. Our challenge as parents and teachers is not to create a spiritual core in their souls but rather to fan the flame of their spiritual core already aglow with the fire of their premortal faith. . . . The stories of Jesus shared over and over bring faith in the Lord Jesus Christ and strength to the foundation of testimony. Can you think of a more valuable gift for our children? Are the life and teachings of Jesus Christ embedded in the minds and souls of our children? Do they think about the Savior's life when they wonder what to do in their own lives? This will be more and more important in the years ahead" (Neil L. Andersen, "Tell Me the Stories of Jesus," *Ensign*, May 2010)

77

*This was 13 years ago!

I DON'T KNOW of any other parenting objective that should take a more prominent place in our quest than that of pointing our children toward the Savior. He and His characteristics are our model in *how* to parent and can be the solution to all the challenges our children face.

Our family has embraced a theme that we hope will be used in family home evenings, reunions, and daily challenges, and perhaps when it comes time for our "transfer" to the next life, they will feel to stand together in our funeral services and recite it. You will find it familiar.

> For we labor diligently to write, to persuade our children, and also our brethren, to believe in Christ, and to be reconciled to God; for we know that it is by grace that we are saved, after all we can do.
>
> And we talk of Christ, we rejoice in Christ, we preach of Christ, we prophesy of Christ, and we write according to our prophecies, that our children may know to what source they may look for a remission of their sins. (2 Nephi 25:23, 26)

It is our hope that along the way our family circle and its subset circles will recognize and embrace Jesus Christ as their Savior, Redeemer, and Exemplar in all things.

Let's imagine we are in a room together and have the blessing of sharing ideas with one another. Suppose our subject is "How can we create a Christ-centered home and point our children to the Savior that they may in fact know to what source they may look for a remission of their sins and understand that it is by grace we are saved, after all we can do?" In other words, "What does Christ-centered parenting look like?" Let me begin a list of ideas:

There is a jar of candy in my home office placed on the highest level of a bookshelf, just above the shelf that contains several sets of worn scriptures I've used over the years. The transparent jar is strategically located so that only a tall grandpa can reach it. Our growing number of grandchildren have come to know where it is and what is required of them to have a piece of its sweet contents. They need to recite a scripture or tell me a scripture story they learned. Then with delight, they see me take down the jar and allow them to take a piece. I can see a pattern developing, and I'm enjoying it.

Our daughter's family was experiencing great challenges and placed a "miracle" or "tender mercies of the Lord" bulletin board in their home. The children were invited to watch for the hand of the Lord in their lives and record it on the wall. This kept them focused on their source of help and bound them together.

General conference is traditionally a family weekend. It is laced with the wonderful aroma of cinnamon rolls, general conference bingo, and "name that speaker." But we also invite pertinent "look for" activities and discuss them over food and treats during the breaks. We identify the one-liner quotes and ideas that become a part of the home décor during the following six months.

It is wonderful for children to grow up understanding that when they are discouraged, about to start a new school year, or need special help, they can request a priesthood blessing from their father or other worthy priesthood holder.

I have observed parents with younger children preparing for the sacrament by showing picture books of Christ. I see them prepare for the sacrament and renewal of covenants by putting away toys or coloring books during the passing of it. Little by little, they teach about how the emblems of this important time turn us to Christ and our covenants. I also notice how most teens put their cell phones away.

Display a picture of President Monson near the TV to serve as a reminder that when a program, movie, or game becomes inappropriate in any way, it's time to turn off the TV or change the channel.

Parents should be up first, engaging in personal scripture study so that when the children wake up, that's the first thing they see. Family scripture time is easier for them to engage in, knowing that it's something Dad and Mom find important. When my ninety-five-year-old mother died, she had read her scriptures that day, and her red pencil was about one and one-half inches long— she had marked every verse in every book of scripture over the years because they were all important.

We found that our teenagers were most ready to talk when they came home at night. I can remember children sitting on the bed or on top of the dresser, talking about their evening or about certain questions or challenges. Whenever a child wants to talk, it is a perfect time to take their "spiritual temperature." Listen, listen, and listen. Talk when you are invited to, but mostly listen. Direct them to the Savior. Ask, "Have you prayed about it?"

Set a tone for the Sabbath. Sunday-appropriate music, activities that honor His day, and dress—while not always Sunday best—should reflect an attitude that is more reverent than other days.

The Church continues to produce extraordinary short videos, Mormon messages, and other resources that can be found at LDS.org or on YouTube. Viewing them one at a time, followed by discussion, is time well invested. Resist spending an hour watching several videos one after another. Rather, keep your children's attention focused on a singular message. Savor the message, focus on a single message, talk about it, and extend an invitation to apply it.

Grandparents can study patriarchal blessings with grandchildren, share stories of family history, write letters to grandchildren serving missions that share testimony, and organize grand family or extended family home evenings.

I am always pleased and comforted when I see pictures and posters of scripture heroes in grandchildren's bedrooms.

When family and friends face challenges, be specific in adding them and their needs to your family prayer.

What are your suggestions? I know flashes of ideas and spiritual nudgings that are customized for your children and family will come to you. The Holy Ghost stands ready to inspire you, and I know the Lord is interested in blessing you in your parenting.

It is well for us to remember who our children are. They are spirit children of God.

Children seem to be drawn to and recognize Christ. Well over a half century ago, President J. Reuben Clark said of the children and youth born into our homes, "[They] are hungry for the things of the Spirit; they are eager to learn the gospel, and they want it straight, undiluted. . . . [They] crave the faith their fathers and mothers have; they want it in its simplicity and purity. . . . You do not have to sneak up behind [them] and whisper religion in [their] ears. . . . You can bring these truths to [them] openly" ("The Charted Course of the Church in Education," *Teaching Seminary Preservice Readings Religion 370, 471, and 475* [Salt Lake City: The Church of Jesus Christ of Latter-day Saints, 2004], 2, 5).

Elder Neil L. Andersen further counsels,

> To fathers and mothers, to grandfathers and grandmothers, and to those without children of their own who lovingly nurture children and youth, my counsel is to speak more frequently about Jesus Christ. In His holy name is great spiritual power.
>
> To mothers who are raising their children without a father in the home, I promise you that as you speak of Jesus Christ, you will feel the power of heaven blessing you. . . .
>
> I make a special appeal to fathers: Please be an important part of talking to your children about the Savior. They need the confirming expressions of your faith, along with those of their mother. ("Tell Me the Stories of Jesus," *Ensign*, May 2010)

Parenting Self-Examination

1. As a parent, take an inventory of your home, children's bedrooms, and story time. Is the focus on Christ and is He appropriately represented?
2. As a grandparent or parent of adult children, what can you do to add your testimony to focus on Jesus? What can you give to

your children or grandchildren to ensure they know how you feel about the centrality of Christ in your life?

3. If you can think of people in your ward or stake who seem to be particularly exemplary in this regard, find an opportunity to ask them what they do to maintain a focus on Christ in their homes. Record their responses in your journal. Consider similar application in your life and home.

Scriptures for Study

| Acts 17:27–28 | D&C 68:25 | 2 Nephi 25:23, 26 |
| 3 Nephi 27:21 | 3 Nephi 18:16 | 1 Nephi 17:55 |

D&C 68:6

A Parting Thought

It is a great responsibility to help our children understand, receive, and maintain Christ as a central figure in their lives. Our efforts need to be natural. We should refrain from becoming zealots or pharisaic in our approaches. Just as pounding on the same piano key can become annoying, so can pounding on the single key of this chapter's message. It is integrating all the keys of the piano into a melody that captures our hearts and minds. Just as a catchy musical tune sticks in our mind, it is seeing and feeling the beauty of Jesus Christ in our lives that will embed Him into the lives of our children. Further, we can only play that melodious tune if we are in harmony ourselves.

Remember: No recipes. Study. Self-examine. Do your best. Live worthy of the Holy Ghost. Pray that the Lord will touch your doings and consecrate them for the blessing and benefit of you, your children, and your grandchildren.

Principle 16 ——————————

Plant Seeds

"Mothers and fathers need to plant the seeds of the gospel firmly in the hearts of their children, to create in them a desire to serve and also to know how to serve—seeds of <u>hard work</u>, seeds of <u>courtesy</u>, seeds of <u>thrift</u>. Then, deep in their hearts, your sons and daughters need to have planted the more valuable seeds of spirituality—the seeds of <u>cleanliness</u>, the seeds of <u>love</u>, the seeds of <u>virtue</u>, the seeds of <u>courage</u>. . . . The seed of <u>obedience</u> is the first law of the gospel and was exemplified by the Savior, who was obedient in all things." (David B. Haight, "Planting Gospel Seeds of Spirituality," *Ensign*, January 1973)

PLANTING SEEDS has always been fascinating to me. Bean, corn, wheat, and watermelon seeds are recognizable and sprout relatively quickly. Spinach, beets, radishes, carrots, and lettuce are less identifiable. Place those seeds in the ground at the proper time of year and under the right circumstances and insure they have appropriate moisture, light, and nutrients. How amazing it is to see them grow and produce a harvest. It's just as interesting, though not welcome, to see how weed seeds sprout and grow as well. They don't require much tending and will grow everywhere if we don't pay attention. A full chapter could be written using this metaphor alone.

Likewise, most of parenting is about "<u>seeds and harvests</u>" and "<u>weeds and control</u>." The trick is making sure we <u>plant seeds we want to harvest</u>, making sure we don't mistake spinach or lettuce for something noxious, and making sure we don't find tumble weeds or thorns where we thought we had tomatoes or squash.

The most obvious seeds we want to plant are the easiest to understand and sow, like prayer, a love for the scriptures, meaningful Church attendance, family home evening, and being kind and Christlike in our behavior. Carefully and consistently nurtured, these will bring a good harvest. Elder Dallin H. Oaks has taught,

> If we are practicing our faith and seeking the companionship of the Holy Spirit, His presence can be felt in our hearts and in our homes. A family having daily family prayers and seeking to keep the commandments of God and honor his name and speak lovingly to one another will have a spiritual feeling in their home that will be discernible to all who enter it. I know this, because I have felt the presence or absence of that feeling in many LDS homes. ("'Always Have His Spirit,'" *Ensign*, November 1996)

The quote at the beginning of this chapter is originated in the context of preparing children to serve missions. As a former mission president, I'd like to comment as an observer on the "harvesting" end of seeds that were planted in homes and families a decade or two earlier. Elder Haight mentions seeds of hard work, courtesy, thrift, and cleanliness. In a mission setting, it was easy to watch the harvest of the seeds of hard work (or the lack thereof in a few missionaries). Courtesy was something Sister Christensen noticed even more than I did; the seeds of thrift or thorns of extravagance bore sweet or sometimes bitter fruit in discernable ways. Cleanliness of mind as well as physical settings was a critical attribute for having the Spirit, and thus having success. I observed that those missionaries who had nurtured the seeds of obedience were blessed with the greatest power and blessings in the work of the Lord.

One day, my cell phone buzzed in my suit pocket. I was awaiting the arrival of a missionary whom I wanted to visit with me. I checked my phone and noticed the name of one of the stake presidents in our mission. Receiving calls from stake presidents outside of our regularly scheduled meeting was seldom good. When those infrequent calls came, there was often a negative reason—a spiritual or physical concern for a missionary. "Buenos dias, presidente," I said, answering the phone.

He was cordial and requested, "President Christensen, I would like to visit with you regarding two of your missionaries." My heart dropped. This was not a good sign. I said, "Okay, who do you need to talk about?" His response stabbed my heart: "No president, I want to come to your office to talk about them in person, face-to-face." I asked him how soon he could be at my office, and he replied that he could be there within a half hour. As I waited for him, I went to the picture board where photos of all our missionaries in companionships were on display, organized by stake. I looked at the pictures of each of those missionaries, asking myself, "Who could it be? Who are the problems?" I scanned the pictures of the ten companionships who worked in the wards of the stake. We had an "obedient" mission, and as I looked at the faces of each missionary, I could not imagine even one being a problem. Confused, I continued to look at the pictures, asking the Lord to help me know who the problem companionship might be and how I could help them.

Soon the stake president arrived. After a cordial Chilean *abrazo* (hug), we walked a few steps over to the board where the pictures of the missionaries in his stake were posted. The stake president looked me straight in the eyes, pointed at the pictures of two missionaries side by side, and said in a kind and confident voice, "President, I don't know which one of these missionaries is Ammon and which one is Aaron, but I am sure they've got to be them!" Ammon and Aaron were two of the greatest missionaries in the Book of Mormon, so I immediately ascertained that this wasn't going to be a negative experience. He repeated, "Seriously, President Christensen, I don't know which is Ammon and which is Aaron, but they are both very special missionaries." Then referring to the board containing nearly two hundred missionaries, he said, "You should be proud of all your missionaries. They are wonderful and effective messengers of the Lord. But these two," he again pointed at the two missionaries being referenced, "these are powerful missionaries."

He went on to relate a personal experience he had the evening before when these two missionaries had come to his home to teach a young couple who were special friends of him and his wife. They had accepted the invitation to receive the first discussion. The president and his wife invited the missionaries to join them at dinner. As a mission, we had discussed the issue of members inviting missionaries to eat dinner, which usually was late getting started, and the result was that an entire evening could be lost waiting for dinner. So our missionaries were taught to discreetly decline and try to zero in on a time frame that would lend itself to not missing out on "prime time" (evening) for teaching others. The stake president said the missionaries had declined, indicating they had another commitment, but they accepted arriving in time for dessert. They suggested to the president that immediately after dessert they could move right into the discussion. It was agreeable.

The stake president said, "Well, we were a little late getting started on dinner so it put us a little behind, but after dessert the missionaries began to teach. Oh President Christensen, they were marvelous! The Spirit was present, they asked wonderful questions and testified in plain and simple words, and I was so excited for our friends, who were also visibly connected to the missionaries." But in the middle of the discussion, the stake president notice the older missionary looking discreetly at his watch. As the older missionary taught and directed the conversation, the newer missionary discreetly checked his watch. "I observed this and then looked at my own watch and understood their concern," he related to me. It was nearly the time designated by the mission as the hour for the missionaries to be in their apartment for the evening. "Oh but President Christensen, the Spirit was so strong! I didn't want them to stop," he related. The stake president asked to meet the missionaries for just a moment in the kitchen. They quickly stepped behind closed doors where the president told the missionaries that he would talk to me about it the next day and let me know the reason for their tardiness getting back to their apartment. He complimented the missionaries and indicated that if they would stay, he would jump in the car and take them home, even though their apartment was just a few blocks away. The two missionaries were quiet at first, then the older companion looked at the president directly in the eyes and said, "President, we are here to serve you and the Lord and share the gospel with your friends. Our mission president, President Christensen, has promised us that if we will be obedient with exactness [Alma 57:21], we will have the power to convert and bless the lives of many, including your friends." Then the president said, with emotion in his eyes, "They asked me, 'President, what do you think we should do?'" "Be obedient," the stake president had answered.

They returned to the living room and proceeded through an abbreviated first discussion, delivering a powerful testimony and witness. The couple was riveted and felt the Spirit. I was emotional as well as I thanked the stake president for this wonderful feedback. "No, I'm not done yet," he said. "There's more." Following an invitation to pray about what they learned that evening and to continue learning in other discussions with a goal of preparing for baptism, an appointment was set. The missionaries courteously thanked the stake president's wife for the dessert and excused themselves. The president accompanied them to the outer street door typical in Latin America. The stake president said to me, "As I said good-bye and closed the door to the street, I could hear the missionaries take off running so that they would arrive to their apartment before they were late." Again I thanked him for sharing the experience, and he said, "No, there's a little bit more. When I returned back into the living room, I explained the need for the missionaries to leave and a little about the schedule of missionaries and their daily life." Then the friend said, "I know we need to learn more about your Church. If your Church produces great people like those two young men, then we want to be a part of it."

"I don't know which is Ammon and which is Aaron, but I'm pretty sure they are them—powerful messengers!"

Now, I wasn't in the homes of these two missionaries when their parents were planting seeds, but I have a feeling that they were learning about obedience, being clean and courteous, and putting their faith and trust in Heavenly Father. I'm confident that if asked how they produced such fine sons, they would answer, "We don't know. We just tried to do the simple things like prayer, scripture time, being kind—those kinds of things."

Be a good sower. Plant, cultivate, and keep the moisture and sunlight just right. You will have an excellent harvest! The Lord has promised it.

Parenting Self-Examination

1. Take a seed inventory. If you are a parent of young children, ask yourself what seeds you are trying to plant.
2. If you are parents of older children, what harvest are you enjoying right now? Is there any weeding that needs to occur? What can you do to cultivate, repent (change), and sow seeds that will bring a better harvest?
3. If you are grandparents, is there anything you can do to make sure you are planting worthy seeds?

Scriptures for Study

Mosiah 4:15   Alma 57:21   Genesis 24:7
Luke 2:52   Galatians 5:13

A Parting Thought

Weed seeds blow in from anywhere, sprout, and take root in almost any soil. If you're not paying attention to the garden, weeds can take over. None of us plant weeds—they just grow and reseed if we allow them to grow mature enough to drop their own seeds. Watch for weeds while you are planting seeds. If you haven't already done it, it would be a good time to check the weeds and either go to work and pull them out by hand or conduct an aggressive and selective herbicide program. Elder Oaks gave a helpful hint to the process of growing the seeds of testimony when he said, "Our children should also hear us bear our testimonies frequently. We should also strengthen our children by encouraging them to define themselves by their growing testimonies, not just by their recognitions in scholarship, sports, or other school activities" ("Testimony," *Ensign*, May 2008).

> Remember: No recipes. Study. Self-examine. Do your best. Live worthy of the Holy Ghost. Pray that the Lord will touch your doings and consecrate them for the blessing and benefit of you, your children, and your grandchildren.

Principle 17

Discipline, a Path to Discipleship

"You may, figuratively speaking, pound one [child] over the head with a club, and he does not know but what you have handed him a straw dipped in molasses to suck. There are others, if you speak a word to them, or take up a straw and chasten them, whose hearts are broken; they are as tender in their feelings as an infant, and will melt like wax before the flame. You must not chasten them severely; you must chasten them according to the spirit that is in the person." (Brigham Young, *Teachings of Presidents of the Church: Brigham Young* [Salt Lake City: The Church of Jesus Christ of Latter-day Saints, 1997], 137–43)

THIS CHAPTER discusses the subject of discipline. There is significant debate about the dos and the don'ts of discipline. I will not attempt to jump into the debate but rather share five principles that may be helpful. In the end, you and the Holy Ghost need to determine your path. If it is Spirit-directed, all will be blessed. The most important principles are the one or two that seem to jump out at you because you are either searching for answers or because you need to adjust something.

Principle One: Avoid anger when disciplining children

Ask yourself every time you administer discipline to your children:

- Am I doing this for my child, or am I doing it for me?
- Is this helpful in solving the problem, or does it just release my emotions?
- What can I do to replace yelling and spanking and control my anger?

It has been my experience that most of the time the kind of discipline we feel bad about doesn't change the problem or fix it long term. It simply lets us release steam. In other words, we are the ones that feel the temporary reward; those receiving punishment or discipline probably aren't as changed by it.

As grandparents and part of the older generation of our ward family, we are quiet observers to the next generation of parents. I'm impressed as we see from our new seats on the sidelines a variety of approaches. In some we observe a great deal of personal control, never raising their voices or reacting harshly. In others we see loving firmness, but always in control of emotions. We see young parents who avoid reacting to a child who explodes in a tantrum, ignoring the outburst but not the child. We observe angry or disobedient children being given a moment in time-out until they can handle their problem in a productive and appropriate way (which also gives the parents a few moments to curb their own anger). We see parents using the principle of distraction to help a child forget the issue that caused the outbreak in the first place.

In one particular instance, I observed a young boy demonstrating open and obvious disobedience to his father's request. Without overreacting, the father asked his son to comply a second time, to which the child looked at his father and continued in his disobedience. After a third request, the little son looked again at his dad and continued without regard to his father's petition. The young and wise father moved in complete emotional control, firmly—without jerking or demonstrating anger—took the child by the hand and started to walk out of the room. At first the little boy resisted, but his stronger father with loving firmness latched on to the boy's arm and walked him through an open door just a few feet into another room. Since the door wasn't closed, I could hear what was going on. I couldn't catch what the father said, but I detected a controlled and caring tone of voice. Questions were asked, followed by responses from his son. The words were not detectable, but I could sense love and firmness. Within one minute, they returned together. The problem was solved, at least on the short term. There was interaction devoid of anger and uncontrolled emotion.

I understand that it can be common to have our emotional fuses lit by these little ones and youth who call us Mom or Dad. It is a part of parenthood. We must control it. We will likely fail on occasion and feel regret. However, I believe that as we seek to avoid anger in our efforts to discipline, the Lord will bless us to succeed more often than we fail. Our children will sense our love, and in time the Lord will consecrate our actions to the best good for our children.

Meanwhile, "pray unto the Father with all the energy of heart, that ye may be filled with this love, which he hath bestowed upon all who are true followers of his Son, Jesus Christ" (Moroni 7:48).

Principle Two: Love is generally the answer

Someone once said, "Love is not an action or a technique. It is a feeling that guides our actions." Love-motivated discipline looks very different from anger-induced punishment. Somehow, when love fills our hearts, we act differently. We want what's best for our children. Brigham Young taught, "Bring up your children in the love and fear of the Lord; study their dispositions and their temperaments, and deal with them accordingly, never allowing yourself to correct them in the heat of passion; teach them to love you rather than to fear you" (*Discourses of Brigham Young*, compiled by John A. Widstoe [Salt Lake City: Deseret Book, 1941], 207).

Truly loving our children and having our relationship built upon love causes us to see them differently. Instead of seeing them as an impediment to our own desires, we see them as an opportunity and gift because we love them. When we act in love, we feel more assistance from the Savior and the Holy Ghost. We like ourselves more in the process. In a loving relationship, we can teach them correct principles without linking them to the bad behavior we are hoping to eliminate.

Our children were a joy and a challenge for their dad, in all the ways your children are a challenge for you. I remember one of my children stole a piece of candy from the store. Another time the bishop came to me and shared some negative information about one of my teens. And another time a child was caught cheating in school. I felt horrible and thought I had taught them better. After I flushed out the prideful feelings about what others might think of me, I distinctly remember being flooded with the love I had in my heart for them. Everything changed. I felt the Savior's love for them and a desire to teach them. I tried to orchestrate or provide an environment for helping them learn about repentance and our Savior. Those were good experiences—for us all, I think.

There is a natural desire in most of us to want and seek for approval from those who love us. In fact, most children depend upon the love and security of their parents. Disapproval with love is more powerful than harsh forms of discipline. In my own life, my parents were not spankers. However, my dad was on occasion

DISCIPLINE, A PATH TO DISCIPLESHIP

a "thumper" (with his thumb on the top of our heads) or an "encourager" (with the side of his size-thirteen foot), but never in a harsh way. Like most parents, they raised their voices on occasion when we certainly deserved it. But a glance or look of disfavor from the loving face of my mother or the quiet caring look of disapproval from my father was enough. Don't you think that's the most effective agent for change Heavenly Father uses with us? When we arrive at a feeling of godly sorrow, we are in a position to change our hearts.

We can and should discipline the way Doctrine and Covenants 121 teaches us: "By persuasion, by long-suffering, by gentleness and meekness, and by love unfeigned; by kindness, and pure knowledge" (verses 41–42).

Principle Three: Be "equally yoked" or unified as parents and always consistent

One parent may not agree on the form of discipline used by the other, but they'd better support each other or the game gets tougher. Spend time discussing it. Avoid argument over differences. My wife and I generally had a periodic get-away trip. We took the opportunity to take inventory of our children and tried to unify our approach in helping each one. Parents must be together on the matter of discipline. We've been blessed by this agreement: if we don't agree on discipline or reaction in the heat of the moment when we are at our worst, we still support each other in the presence of our children and then discussed it later in private. The errant one always knows what was out of bounds. In private, more often than not, it's been a time to regroup and support each other in more appropriate actions in the future. Elder Oaks teaches, "The father presides and has the ultimate responsibility the government of the home, but parenting is obviously a shared responsibility. Both parents occupy a leading role in teaching their children, and both must counsel together and support one another. . . . In the sacred task of teaching the children of God, parents should unite and combine their efforts to dispel the powers of darkness from the lives of their children" ("Parental Leadership in the Family," *Ensign*, June 1985, 9).

Seek to be consistent in whatever pattern of discipline you embrace. Waffling or changing will become confusing to children. Help children to know that actions have consequences. Teach them through consistency which actions bring positive results and which produce negative outcomes. Consistency in your inspired methods of discipline will bless your children.

Principle Four: Remember, agency is the fundamental principle of life on earth

From a very early age, we display the fundamental principle upon which our life operates—agency. We want and flourish in free will. The greatest challenge of any parent is to somehow maintain order and appropriate control while respecting and nurturing this God-given power to choose. Avoid contention, power struggles, and domination. We can work with agency rather than against it by learning to give choices that help guide in the right direction. As near as I can tell, agency is the right to choose the right. When we choose wrongly, our agency is diminished. Giving children choices between two rights helps them eliminate any desire to make the wrong choices along the way.

Principle Five: Build vision and promote learning

Create a vision in the family that we can learn from our negative choices. We can look back at moments when we weren't at our best or made decisions that required correction and learn from them. We can ask each other, "What did we learn from all that chaos that happened yesterday when we all got upset?" Help the family to see that we are a project and on a journey to becoming better. Engage all who are old enough to talk and reason. Older children especially need to feel that we are on a journey together and we can learn from each other in our quest to become a forever family. *Discipline* has the same root word as *discipleship*. Discipleship is the basis for our coming to and following the Savior. Help each to understand and remember that we are in this together.

Parenting Self-Examination

1. Did you experience any nudges or stirrings in the process of reading this chapter? Any promptings for change?
2. Think of the experiences in your childhood. Focus on any and all good aspects of the discipline your parents administered. As you consider any actions that were not appropriate, what are you doing or what have you done to break those negative practices so they will not be perpetuated in the next generation?
3. Communicate with your spouse and determine future improvement.

Scriptures for Study

> 1 Nephi 8:37   Moroni 7:48   D&C 121:41–42
> Proverbs 13:24 → Mosiah 4:14

A Parting Thought

President Gordon B. Hinckley, in speaking of correction, reminded us,

> The Lord, in setting forth the spirit of governance in his Church, has also set forth the spirit of governance in the home in these great words of revelation: "No power or influence can or ought to be maintained . . . only by persuasion, by long-suffering, by gentleness and meekness, and by love unfeigned; reproving betimes with sharpness, when moved upon by the Holy Ghost; then showing forth afterwards an increase of love toward him whom thou hast reproved, lest he esteem thee to be his enemy; that he may know that thy faithfulness is stronger that the cords of death." . . . There is no discipline in all the world like the discipline of love. It has a magic all its own." ("The Environment of Our Homes," *Ensign*, June 1985, 6)

> Remember: No recipes. Study. Self-examine. Do your best. Live worthy of the Holy Ghost. Pray that the Lord will touch your doings and consecrate them for the blessing and benefit of you, your children, and your grandchildren.

Principle 18 ———————————————

Balancing What's Important

"I find some of our brethren who are engaged in some leadership position justify their neglect of their family because they say that they are engaged in the Lord's work. I say to them, 'My dear brother, do you realize that the most important part of the Lord's work that you will do is the work that you do within the walls of your own home?' That is the most important work of the Lord. Don't get your sense of values mixed up." (Harold B. Lee, BYU Speeches, April 19, 1961, 5)

OVER HALF a century ago, President Harold B. Lee made the above statement. A few years later, President David O. McKay coined the oft quoted proclamation, "No other success can compensate for failure in the home" (Conference Report, April 1935, 116). Today it is commonplace for both men and women to allow their values to stray from home and family. Someone once said that we will spend our time and energy on that which we most value. When I first heard that statement, I didn't agree. I could think of a lot of things I was required to do that I valued much less than the things I wanted to do and valued much more. However, I'm finding more and more that there is substance to that notion.

The combined counsel given by these two great prophets, seers, and revelators provides the bedrock upon which we must consider our most important roles—our marriages and parent-hood. The Lord Himself said, "And again, inasmuch as parents have children in Zion, or in any of her stakes which are organized, that teach them not to understand the doctrine of repentance, faith in Christ the Son of the living God, and of baptism and the gift of the Holy Ghost by the laying on of the hands, when eight years old, the sin be upon the heads of the parents" (D&C 68:25).

Other prophets have given additional counsel:

> The question is sometimes asked by younger priesthood hold-ers, "Where do I place my greatest priorities—to the Church, to my family, or to my profession?" I have answered that ques-tion be emphasizing that heads of families have four major responsibilities. Certainly the first is to the home and family. There should be no question about this. A man may succeed in business or his Church calling, but if he fails in his home he will face eternity in disappointment. . . . Home is the place where the Lord intended a father's greatest influence to be felt. (Ezra Taft Benson, *Teachings of Ezra Taft Benson* [Salt Lake City: Bookcraft, 1988], 509–10)

> We counsel parents and children to give highest priority to family prayer, family home evening, gospel study and instruc-tion, and wholesome family activities. However worthy and appropriate other demands or activities may be, they must not be permitted to displace the divinely appointed duties that only parents and families can adequately perform. ("Keeping Chil-dren Close to the Church," in News of the Church, *Ensign*, June 1999)

I think most of my readers would agree that parenting and family matters are of prime importance. We need not spend more time building that case. The greater question is how do we prior-itize our time? What can we do to make sure we don't mix up our values? With all the things that demand our attention, how do we stay focused on the priorities and not get distracted by those things that scream for our attention?

I don't know of any other way than to take time to think and ponder about it. We have to know and confirm what we value the most. I've spent a portion of my professional life helping others identify their values. Everyone thinks they know what they value, but in every setting in which I've consulted, there have been hazy interpretations at best of what people value. I will often ask a group of individuals to suppose they received information from their doctor tomorrow morning that they have a health situation that will likely not slow them down until the last two to three weeks of their lives, but that they have at best four months to live. I ask them if they would do anything different in the next three months than they did in the last three months. I invite you to do the same exercise. Think about it. How would you live the next ninety days, knowing that in a one hundred and twenty days your spirit would be transferred to the spirit world. Where would you spend your time? What would you do differently?

In that context, I ask them to write down the most important things in their lives. At first they focus their attention on creating their list. One or two things come quickly and often they pause and don't write down any more. Most, in or out of the Church, will identify that family, spouses, or children are their greatest priorities. God and church make the list. I've yet to find anyone who has identified their business or employment to be their highest priority. Yet our careers, professions, hobbies, past times, social media, sports, movies, and video games take the biggest chunk of time. We will address the subject of time in another chapter. This much I will say, if we don't know what we clearly value, we will find that the things we care about the most get crowded out.

Once you know, take time to think about it everyday. President Gordon B. Hinckley once counseled the members of the Church to "take a little time to meditate, to think" ("A Time of New Beginnings," *Ensign*, May 2000). Thinking and pondering opens channels to the Spirit, which will teach us all things we should do. It is a simple thing to do, but it does require consistency. In a day, 1 percent is 14.4 minutes. Maybe we could invest 1 percent of our day to pondering and thinking.

I can predict that if we do take the time to identify our values in writing and then spend fourteen to fifteen minutes each day considering how well we are paying attention to those values, then we will feel more content that we are living a balanced life. It will mean you will say no to some things and spend a little more time on others. But if we don't, then I also predict with confidence that life will go on pretty much the same as it has in the past, which often means family gets crowded out by other things of lesser value.

Take time to think! Then focus on the family, your parenting, and your kids.

Parenting Self-Examination

1. Do your actions and focus correlate with what you value the most?
2. Where do you need to adjust so that you are keeping your priorities and values straight?
3. Family matters are the most important part of your life. Plan your next work week with that in mind, figuring out ways to make sure you keep balance and pay attention to your family.

Scriptures for Study

Matthew 6:33 34   Mosiah 4:27   Alma 34:32
1 Timothy 5:8   Timothy 3:5

A Parting Thought

Balancing values and giving appropriate time and energy to all the important areas of our lives is a real exercise in juggling or plate spinning. I know that Heavenly Father knows we need to work to provide for our families. He also asks us to serve in His kingdom in callings that take time. I know that He knows we live in communities that need us to serve our fellow man. I therefore know that He will bless us with the ability to do what we need to do to give our highest priorities and values proper attention.

> Remember: No recipes. Study. Self-examine. Do your best. Live worthy of the Holy Ghost. Pray that the Lord will touch your doings and consecrate them for the blessing and benefit of you, your children, and your grandchildren.

Principle 19

Time

"Obviously, family values mirror our personal priorities. Given the gravity of current conditions, would parents be willing to give up just one outside thing, giving that time and talent instead to the family? Parents and grandparents, please scrutinize your schedules and priorities in order to ensure that life's prime relationships get more prime time!" (Neal A Maxwell, "'Take Especial Care of Your Family,'" *Ensign*, May 1994)

RECENTLY, AFTER spending the day working on projects, answering emails, and making telephone calls, I looked out the window of my office and saw two little boys sitting on the front steps of their home. They seemed to be engaged in deep discussion about something. I know the two: Landon, age eight, and Carter, age five. They call me Grandpa. I wondered if they were talking about ants or maybe sharks; Landon's latest childhood dream is to someday be a marine biologist and study hammerheads. Carter on the other hand is more interested in being in charge now and running his household. "We are really blessed to be living across the street from them," I mused.

After a few minutes, they jumped up and ran into their house. "Well, I'd better get back to finishing these last two or three tasks on my list," I said to myself just as I saw another grandson, Jacob (age twelve), walk out of his home. He slumped down and occupied the same seat on the front steps where his two younger brothers had been a minute or two before. His posture sent a message that he and his older sister, Kylee (age fourteen), must have just had a normal sibling encounter of who really is in charge of everything when Mom and Dad are gone. Their parents were out of town on professionally related matters and my wife was also out of town taking care of one of our daughters who would soon give birth. I was tasked with "just keeping a watch on them" from across the street while their parents were out of town. Exactly what I was doing, right? Watching them! Taylor, age sixteen, was at his job and wouldn't return until 8:00 p.m. "I'm just about through with these last two items on my to-do list," I reminded myself and started to turn away from my lookout duty back to the tasks at hand.

The sight of Jacob's slumped shoulders and bowed head staring at the sidewalk interrupted me one more time. Watching that great deacon sitting there alone spawned two thoughts that popped into my head nearly simultaneously. The first was the words of my son, the father of the five kids who were home alone for the week: "Yeah, Jacob is having a problem with his new parents (the two older siblings) and as the guy in the middle of two little happy-go-lucky brothers and two authorities, he'll struggle a little while we're gone." About then he picked up a stick and started poking it in the flowerbed in front of him. The second thought flashed into the main stage of my mind, one that has entered that stage hundreds of times: "The moments of highest positive impact in my children's (and grandchildren's) lives come to me in the most inconvenient moments." Then the internal dialogue began. "Yeah, but I've got just two more things on my list!" I responded to myself. "I'll do something with him later in the evening. He'll soon get over whatever bothering him. He always does." Again the thought returned: "The moments of highest positive impact in my children's (and grandchildren's) lives come to me in the most inconvenient moments."

I caved in. I got up, quickly went into our garage, opened the door, and pulled my bright green convertible "grandpa jeep wrangler" into my driveway. Being just across the street, Jacob saw me pull out of the garage. He got up from his brooding perch on the front step of his house and started walking across the street like a fish moving toward tantalizing bait. "Wanna go for a ride?" I asked. "Sure," he quickly replied. Then he asked, "Can we take the doors off, Grandpa?" "Absolutely, I was just thinking the same thing," I answered.

Jacob and I went for a ride. We stopped at Ace Hardware to pick up a couple of things on my list for the next day's yard work. We drove around town and up by the Rexburg Temple, talking about life, friends, his upcoming seventh grade year, and his ordinal position in the family circle. He opened right up and started telling some of his feelings about how he felt his life was a little miserable. After listening for a while, I empathized with him, telling him about my days at home with five older and three younger siblings. "You know, Jake, I think I felt the same way," I said. I told him how proud I was of him. I told him that I loved hearing his testimony nearly every fast Sunday and how much he reminded me of his dad (whom I know he loves). It was a good summer afternoon for both of us. Then another thought popped into my mind. "How about we go pick up Kylee, Landon, and Carter and go for an early pizza dinner? I know your mom has all your food prepared for the week, but hey, what do you think?" Jacob smiled, showing excellent orthodontics work. When we pulled into his driveway, I suggested, "Go in the house and tell the others where we are going." Jacob started to get out and then stopped. He leaned over, looking me in the eyes, gave me a "man hug," and said, "Thanks, Grandpa!" He went into the house to invite the others to the pizza party.

The other kids ran out of the house, and we drove away to a great all-you-can-eat buffet at Pizza Pie Cafe. When we left the restaurant, the last two items on my list at my home office started screaming at me again. "Gotta get back and get those things done!" But I was feeling good and the thought that saved me the first time entered my mind again, this time more subtle but still clear: "The moments of highest positive impact in my children's (and grandchildren's) lives come to me in the most inconvenient moments." Instead of turning at the stoplight to go back home, I continued straight. "Where you going, Grandpa?" Landon asked. "Let's take the long road home," I answered.

Not far from our home, I entered a dirt road my wife and I had discovered on our early morning walks. It wasn't far from our homes, but the kids hadn't been on it. It was a steep incline that dropped down into a little valley. It was a bumpy, dusty road that wound around through the trees with a steep hill on one side and a wheat field on the other. With the doors off the jeep, to Carter and Landon it seemed like we were on a safari. "This is awesome, Grandpa," "This is the best day ever," "I wish Taylor was here," and another dozen affirmations confirmed that "the moments of highest positive impact in my children's (and grandchildren's) lives come to me in the most inconvenient moments." A few minutes later I asked, "Shall I drop you guys off at your house, or would you like to go to Chevron to get some gas?" It was quick and unanimous: "We want to go with you." A few minutes later, with a full tank of gas and five small pieces of candy I had bought and distributed, we drove home. It was a wonderful ninety minutes. They piled out of the green jeep with "I love you, Grandpa," "Thanks, Grandpa," and "You're the best, Grandpa!" That was the right thing to do. And I still got those two last tasks on my list completed.

The experience helped me to remember that at one point in my life as a young father, I was struggling to keep things in balance. Task lists were dominating my life! My kids were growing up, and I'm sure my wife felt alone at times. I knew what was most important but had a hard time finding the ability to do more about the things I valued the most. So the phrase was born and committed to memory and has helped me many, many times: "The moments of highest positive impact in my children's lives come to me in the most inconvenient moments."

I've come home some late afternoons wanting to kick off my shoes and read the morning newspaper. After all, I should be entitled to that, right? But Devin or Candra would come into the room just as I got started reading and ask me for some attention. At first I felt a surge of frustration, followed by, "The moments of highest positive impact in my children's lives come to me in the most inconvenient moments." I would then set the newspaper to the side and listen with my eyes and my ears. Forty-five seconds later, they would leave to go play outside. Reading the newspaper was so much more fulfilling because I had paid attention to something that mattered most first.

On other days in different settings, Chenae would come to me when I was starting on some important task and ask, "Dad, wanna shoot some hoop?" At first, getting my task done always seemed like the right thing to do—after all, "work first, play later" we are taught. But then "The moments of highest positive impact in my children's lives come to me in the most inconvenient moments" came into my mind. While living in Florida, we had just returned from a ward party at the beach. It was late, we were all tired, and the next morning was coming quickly. Chelise said, "Dad, I left my new shoes at the beach." Amidst the grumbling chatter of my inner voice, a familiar thought wiggled into the self-talk conversation: "The moments of highest positive impact in my children's lives come to me in the most inconvenient moments." The round-trip forty-five-minute ride, the one-on-one conversation, and finding the shoes in the location precisely where she left them was the right thing to do. Stories could be shared about when Creshel needed to talk about the drama of teenage friendships, or when Chalonn needed to be assured during changing times, or Aaron always being in a "little hot water" with his mom in early years of his life, or Chantel's disabilities seeming to always call out for attention. In many cases, "The moments of highest positive impact in my children's lives come to me in the most inconvenient moments" has rescued me from my to-do lists and reminded me to act on those things that I valued the most.

I've concluded that children's fun barometers are at the highest when they are spending time with their parents. I've also bought into the notion that "love is spelled T-I-M-E." Those of us who think we can somehow plan quality time to compensate for quantity time are likely in for a surprise. No doubt, quality time is important, and we can engineer some moments that can be impactful. But the greatest love we can show to our children is to respond spontaneously to as many quantity moments as possible.

Elder Dallin H. Oaks in a recent general conference taught, "We have to forego some good things in order to choose others that are better or best because they develop faith in the Lord Jesus Christ and strengthen our families" ("Good, Better, Best," *Ensign*, November 2007, 107).

There are many wonderful electronic devices and apps that give us timely reminders to increase our productivity. If we use these gadgets effectively, our productivity can increase. It stands to reason that life should run a lot more smoothly.

President Dieter F. Uchtdorf counseled,

> Let's be honest; it is rather easy to be busy. We all can think up a list of tasks that will overwhelm our schedules. Some might even think that their self-worth depends on the length of their to-do list. They flood the open spaces in their time with lists

of meetings and minutia. . . . Because they unnecessarily complicate their lives, they often feel increased frustration, diminished joy, and too little sense of meaning in their lives. . . . My dear brothers and sisters, we would do well to slow down a little, proceed at the optimum speed for our circumstances, focus on the significant, lift up our eyes, and truly see the things that matter most. . . . Let us simplify our lives a little. Let us make the changes necessary to refocus our lives on the sublime beauty of the simple, humble path of Christian discipleship—the path that leads always toward a life of meaning, gladness, and peace. ("Of Things That Matter Most," *Ensign*, November 2010)

Parenting Self-Examination

1. How are you doing with the things that matter most?
2. Will you consider giving something up to bring more balance into your life, with a goal of devoting more time to your family?
3. Do you sense the need to change anything? If so, how will you do it?

Scriptures for Study

Ecclesiastes 3:1–8	1 Peter 3:17	Luke 18:22
1 Corinthians 12:31	Ether 12:11	2 Nephi 25:26

A Parting Thought

May we each be blessed to seize those spontaneous moments, planned activities, and all the time we can to spend with our children so that we communicate the love we feel for them. Build memories, laugh, have fun, and do what you can with your circumstances and season of life.

Remember: No recipes. Study. Self-examine. Do your best. Live worthy of the Holy Ghost. Pray that the Lord will touch your doings and consecrate them for the blessing and benefit of you, your children, and your grandchildren.

Principle 20 ——————————————————————

How We Love Each Other

"How can a father raise a happy, well-adjusted [child] in today's increasingly toxic world? The answer has been taught by the Lord's prophets. It is a simple answer, and it is true—'The most important thing a father can do for his [children] is to love [their] mother.' By the way you love [their] mother, you will teach your [children] about tenderness, loyalty, respect, compassion, and devotion. [They] will learn from your example what to expect from [others] and what qualities to seek in a future spouse. You can show your [children] by the way you love and honor your wife that [they] should never settle for less. Your example will teach your [children] to value womanhood. You are showing [them] that [they are children] of our Heavenly Father, who loves [them]." (Elaine Dalton, "Love Her Mother," *Ensign*, November 2011)

I WOULD ADD to Sister Dalton's counsel that the opposite is true. The greatest thing a mother can do to raise a happy, well-adjusted child is to love and support their father. I am grateful that I never wondered even once in my life whether or not my dad loved my mother or my mother loved my dad. I knew they didn't always agree, and it was easy to see that in many ways they were two distinct and different people with varied interests. I sensed a few times that they were having a little tiff when my mother struggled to balance the checkbook or dad needed to finish something that required "just a minute" and it took an hour. There were never any cross words, yelling, or actions that made me wonder if they loved each other. I knew they were each other's best friends.

It is interesting to note the teachings of several Church leaders regarding how important it is to exhibit love for one another. Consider the following counsel:

President Howard W. Hunter

I wish to speak of the relationship that a man holding the priesthood should have with his wife and children. . . . A man who holds the priesthood shows perfect moral fidelity to his wife and gives her no reason to doubt his faithfulness. A husband is to love his wife with all his heart and cleave unto her and none else. . . . You should express regularly to your wife and children your reverence and respect for her. Indeed, one of the greatest things a father can do for his children is to love their mother. . . . A man who holds the priesthood accepts his wife as a partner in the leadership of the home and family with full knowledge of and full participation in all decisions relating thereto. . . . Presiding in righteousness necessitates a shared responsibility between husband and wife; together you act with knowledge and participation in all family matters. For a man to operate independent of or without regard to the feelings and counsel of his wife in governing the family is to exercise unrighteous dominion. . . . Keep yourselves above any domineering or unworthy behavior. ("Being a Righteous Husband and Father," *Ensign*, November 1994)

Elder Delbert L. Stapley

If parents are immature and cannot settle their differences without anger, fighting, and name-calling, a child becomes most insecure, and as he grows older he is apt to take up with the wrong type of friends just to get away from an unhappy home environment. (In Conference Report, October 1970, 45)

Elder Marvin J. Ashton

Often parents communicate most effectively with their children by the way they listen to and address each other. Their conversations showing gentleness and love are heard by our ever-alert, impressionable children. We must learn to communicate effectively not only by voice, but by tone, feeling, glances, mannerisms, and total personality. Too often when we are not able to converse with a daughter or wife we wonder, "What is wrong with her?" when we should be wondering, "What is wrong with our methods?" A meaningful smile, an appropriate pat on the shoulder, and a warm handshake are all-important. Silence isolates. Strained silent periods cause wonderment, hurt, and, most often, wrong conclusions. ("Family Communications," *Ensign*, May 1976, 53)

Elder LeGrand Curtis

Perhaps the best gift parents can give their children is to love each other, to enjoy each other, and even to hold hands and demonstrate their love by the manner in which they talk to each other. Home should be a happy place because all work to keep it that way. It is said that happiness is homemade, and we should endeavor to make our homes happy and pleasant places for us and our children. A happy home is one centered around the teachings of the gospel. This takes constant, careful effort by all concerned. ("Happiness Is Homemade," *Ensign*, November 1990)

Elder Robert D. Hales

It helps children to see that good parents can have differing opinions, and that these differences can be worked out without striking, yelling, or throwing things. They need to see and feel calm communication with respect for each other's viewpoints so they themselves will know how to work through differences in their own lives. ("How Will Our Children Remember Us?" *Ensign*, November 1993)

There is value and importance in the counsel given by these leaders. I am reminded of two students in a class discussion who gave contrasting memories of how their parents treated one another. One said something like, "I recall cold feelings with my parents. Dad was always busy, usually away from home. He seldom called to let my mother know that he would be getting home late from work. Mom would retaliate by having a lot of days when she retired to her bedroom with headaches. Sometimes they would fight with words, but mostly they won their respective battles by silence. I think they loved each other. I'm not sure. I mostly think they didn't like each other."

The other gave this contrasting statement (paraphrasing to the best of my recollection), "My mother was athletic, energetic, and a little crazy, and my dad was academic, quiet, and a little boring. My mother loved to participate in sports, knew who was winning the World Cup playoffs, and knew the passing statistics of everyone who passed through BYU's quarterback factory. My dad preferred a book, enjoyed quiet time in his shift office in our home, knew anything and everything about the history of the world, and rarely spoke in any tone except monotone. Mom loved to spend money, and Dad loved to saved it. Mom was religious to be social, and Dad was religious to be right and good. In short, my parents were as different as night and day. But interestingly, they were best friends. I could never figure that out. How could two people so different like each other so much? We kids would sometime catch them kissing in the kitchen. Other times they would go for a walk together or a long ride. They both liked ice cream, holding hands, teasing one another, and laughing. I noticed they loved kissing and making up after a disagreement more than they liked to win their point of view. My mom and dad loved, liked, and adored each other. I'm more like my mom. My sisters and younger brother are more like my dad. I'm now dating the perfect girl of my dreams, and she's a lot like my dad. I love knowing how two polar opposites can have such a happy marriage."

Parenting Self-Examination

1. Do your children know that you love your spouse? How do they know that? List the ways. Share them with your spouse.
2. Ask your children (if they are old enough) to tell you how they know that you love each other?
3. Take the opportunity to consciously and conspicuously do something every day or week that will show your children that you love your spouse. Make sure its visible.
4. Write a note to your spouse enumerating the reasons why you love her or him. Share it with the whole family at your next family home evening.

Scriptures for Study

| Genesis 2:24 | Proverbs 31:28 | 1 Peter 4:8 |
| Ephesians 5:25–28 | Colossians 3:19–21 | 1 Peter 3:7 |

A Parting Thought

Loving each other as husband and wife is a great gift to our children. It is easy to run parallel lives in achieving our separate roles and to allow ourselves to grow apart or out of "like." Even though we love each other, keeping our "like" for one another is part of becoming and maintaining our success as parents. Work at being eternally appealing to each other. That gift to your children is more important than anything tangible you can give them. Give it daily!

Remember: No recipes. Study. Self-examine. Do your best. Live worthy of the Holy Ghost. Pray that the Lord will touch your doings and consecrate them for the blessing and benefit of you, your children, and your grandchildren.

Principle 21

A Happy Home

"Happy homes come in a variety of appearances. Some feature large families with father, mother, brothers, and sisters living together in a spirit of love. Others consist of a single parent with one or two children, while other homes have but one occupant. There are, however, identifying features which are to be found in a happy home, whatever the number or description of its family members. I refer to these as 'Hallmarks of a Happy Home.' They consist of: 1. A pattern of prayer. 2. A library of learning. 3. A legacy of love. 4. A treasury of testimony." (Thomas S. Monson, "Hallmarks of a Happy Home," *Ensign*, October 2001)

I AM GRATEFUL when I think of the houses on South Lorena and North Glade Road in Farmington, New Mexico, where the Vaughn and Irene Christensen family resided for nearly three decades. They were the kind of homes described by President Monson. I pray that the houses once occupied by our family in Utah, Arizona, Michigan, Florida, and Idaho are homes where our children have treasures of positive memories and feelings of gratitude.

Our prophet quoted "The Family: A Proclamation to the World" to establish the further understanding of the Lord's expectation for creating a happy home: "Happiness in family life is most likely to be achieved when founded upon the teachings of the Lord Jesus Christ. Successful marriages and families are established and maintained on the principles of faith, prayer, repentance, forgiveness, respect, love, compassion, work, and wholesome recreational activities" (*Ensign*, November 1995, 102).

Further, he quoted one of England's great prime ministers who once pronounced, "The family is the building block of society. It is a nursery, a school, a hospital, a leisure center, a place of refuge, and a place of rest. It encompasses the whole of the society. It fashions our beliefs; it is the preparation for the rest of our life" (Nicolas Wood, "Thatcher Champions the Family," *London Times*, 26 May 1988).

Finally, as the presiding high priest of our planet, he has defined the hallmarks, characteristics, and distinctive features that will maximize the probability that our children will love the houses they call home. Let's review them.

A Pattern of Prayer

Prayer is a form of work. I wrote in *Power of Prayer—31 Teachings to Strengthen Our Connection with Heaven* that our connection with heaven is primary and fundamental to our spirituality. Our prayer life is the barometer of our spiritual life. Family prayer, therefore, is a key indicator of the spiritual condition of our family. Two parents connected with heaven will do things far more right in their parenting than they do wrong. Father in Heaven stands ready to answer our concerns, inspire us, and support us in raising His children.

Once, before cell phones, my wife and I were gone from our home one evening for a few hours, leaving our children with a babysitter. Someone accidently locked the baby in the master bedroom. There was a flurry of concern and expressions of doom. Creshel, our seven-year-old daughter, knew of only one answer to the dilemma. She organized her younger siblings and invited the babysitter to kneel for a prayer. She uttered words that calmed everyone, including the crying baby in the locked room. While I don't recall how they found a solution to unlock the door, they did.

As we were finishing our second of three years in Chile, one of our daughters graduated from high school and was making plans to return to the United States to attend college. This meant that our youngest son would be left alone to attend high school during the final year of our service. To add to the impending loss of his older sister, there was a large group of expatriates—whose parents were working for US corporations, the embassy, and in Church assignments—who were leaving too. Our son felt that everyone was leaving him behind and that he would have a lonely year. He approached me one day saying, "Dad, I think I want to go home early." He had even talked to one of his best friends in our home-town whose parents indicated that he could stay with them. I listened and asked him if he'd prayed about it. He indicated he had and would continue to, but he felt sure it was the right thing to do. I invited him to remember that the Lord had called us on the mission and that we could trust the Lord to help us through this question. "Let's give the Lord a chance to answer your concern." Within a few weeks, we began to learn that two new mission presidents who were coming to the Santiago South and West Missions were bringing a total of a dozen children. Two or three other North American families also relocated from the United States to our ward. What had seemed like an impossible situation was reversed when the Lord manifested His hand and gave a sixteen-year-old boy a tender mercy. Trust the Lord.

Since prayer is so important, it's one of the first points of Lucifer's attack to ruin family solidarity and our parenting success. We get too busy to pray together. We get distracted. Multiple schedules and doing multiple good things often rob us of a strong family prayer life.

Elder Hales has reminded us that if we want to talk to God, we pray. If we want God to talk to us, we read the scriptures

(Robert D. Hales, "Holy Scriptures: The Power of God unto Our Salvation," *Ensign*, November 2006). Family scripture time completes the prayer process. More than once, our family has prayed for answers to a particular question or has struggled in some specific area of family living and it was in our reading of a few verses each day that we stumbled across an answer that provided us with an opportunity to discuss its application.

President Spencer W. Kimball stated in simple terms, "Prayer is the passport to spiritual power" (*Teachings of Presidents of the Church: Spencer W. Kimball* [Salt Lake City: The Church of Jesus Christ of Latter-day Saints, 2006], 46–58).

A Library of Learning

I am blessed by an extraordinary father-in-law. My wife remembers many times asking heartfelt and teen-troubling questions of her dad. His response was consistent. He would walk to the family library of good books, scan the titles, pull one from the shelf, open its cover, and then invite her to read from the book. His love for books and prophetic perspective blessed his children as they grew older.

Now my wife collects and displays in artful and fashionable décor quotes from our prophets' general conference teachings. She keeps them fresh with each new conference.

My own father quoted often from a book in our library entitled *Law of the Harvest*. Since he was a farmer most of his life, it was something he related to and taught us from.

In this information age, books are being replaced by millions of options online. I know a young family whose dinner discussions center around digital and video content found on LDS.org or mormon.org. When challenges come up in the family or a child has a concern, like my father-in-law, this young father pulls up a Mormon Message or YouTube video produced by the Church to help his children deal with their concerns.

Every home has to have a library. It may be few volumes or a thousand. Our electronic world has opened up the possibility of a library with millions of volumes and even provides search engines that allow us to have everything from summaries to consolidated studies on every subject imaginable. We can listen to audio books as we go to and from work or as we fly in planes around the earth. We can learn new languages and find almost any answer to any question we have. The information highway is rich with information.

Our library must include the scriptures. In addition, every Latter-day Saint home should have in their library fresh monthly copies of the *Friend, New Era, Ensign,* and even fresher, the weekly *Church News.* Having these available and sharing insights from them will strengthen our homes.

All parents should ensure their homes have a library. Heavenly Father Himself states, "And as all have not faith, seek ye diligently and teach one another words of wisdom; yea, seek ye out of the best books words of wisdom; seek learning, even by study and also by faith" (D&C 88:118).

President Monson added a footnote to his encouragement by reminding us that "our lives may be the book from the family library which the children most treasure. Are our examples worthy of emulation?" ("Hallmarks of a Happy Home," *Ensign,* October 2001).

A Legacy of Love

A home where love is not only spoken about but is shown in daily deeds is sure to become evidence of this characteristic. We are all witnesses of how the power of love can change anything from mediocrity to something or someone incredibly special.

David O. McKay once said, "True Christianity is love in action" (*Teachings of Presidents of the Church: David O. McKay* [Salt Lake City: The Church of Jesus Christ of Latter-day Saints, 2011] 178–85).

Edwin Markham wrote a poem I heard spoken often in my home. I was encouraged by my mother in one of our homemade bread chats to memorize it.

He drew a circle that shut me out—
Heretic, a rebel, a thing to flout.
But Love and I had will to win:
We drew a circle that took him in.
(Edwin Markham, 1852–1940, "Outwitted")

I look at the examples of those around me who are developing a "legacy of love" in their families:

- I see a talented sister who has written lyrics and music to a family song entitled "Family Ties."
- I see a family who was potentially divided by one member who has chosen an alternative lifestyle. Wise parents have taught their family, "We will not let anything affect our love for each other."
- I see a mother who loves her children through the food she provides, the smell of homemade bread, and the taste of home.
- I see a mother who loves through doing acts of service every day.
- I see loving fathers everywhere who love by sacrificing and working hard every day to provide for their families.
- I am impressed that for over fifty years one family has left behind the legacy of love through annual family reunions where they gather for fun, food, and faith. These are valued times when cousins stay connected, brothers and sister bolster and edify each other, and parents feel the joy of seeing the rising generation following the Lord.
- I see a mother who feeds the neighbor friends and makes her home a place where not only her own children love to be but also where others enjoy everything from waffles to popcorn.

A legacy is defined as a *bequest, inheritance, endowment,* or *gift* that is handed down by a predecessor. One of the greatest things we can give to our family is a legacy of love.

A Treasury of Testimony

It's one thing to have a strong testimony; it's another to make sure our children have every opportunity to discover and strengthen theirs in our homes. It is in the home that children catch the flame of a living witness and testimony of the Savior. It's in the home that we understand how to feel about spiritual matters.

In Doctrine and Covenants 46, we learn about the gifts of the Spirit:

> For all have not every gift given unto them; for there are many gifts, and to every man is given a gift by the Spirit of God.
>
> To some is given one, and to some is given another, that all may be profited thereby.
>
> To some it is given by the Holy Ghost to know that Jesus Christ is the Son of God, and that he was crucified for the sins of the world.
>
> To others it is given to believe on their words, that they also might have eternal life if they continue faithful. (Verses 11–14)

I was blessed to be in a home where there was a treasury of testimony. I am grateful for stories that were shared about my great-grandparents who joined the Church and were willing to sacrifice for the gospel's sake. My grandparents were good, faithful people, and in turn Mom and Dad were as true to their testimonies and covenants as anyone ever could be. But I had to get my own testimony and could not ride on the coattails of my parents. I don't ever recall not believing the Church was true, that Joseph was a prophet, or that the Book of Mormon was true. I've always believed. I was the benefactor of one of the gifts of the Spirit, and I believe that gift is almost as universally given as is the Light of Christ. Look at verses 13 and 14 again: "To some it is given . . . to *know*. . . . To others it is given to *believe on their words*." I count it one of the greatest blessings of my life to have been raise in a home where I heard the stories of Jesus and gazed at pictures of Book of Mormon stories. I heard stories of the Mormon pioneers, knowing that my great-grandparents were a part of all that. I heard stories of their conversions and the miracles they witnessed. I was reminded that my own two hands, which were to be amputated from a tragic burning, were preserved through the power of the priesthood. Hundreds of bedtime stories and family home evenings featured the witnesses and tender mercies of the Lord in our life and home.

On that foundation, mine was the gift to believe on their words. At age seventeen, at a most unsuspecting moment during sacrament meeting, a Primary children's choir sang to the congregation "I Am a Child of God." For some reason, I was ready. My belief was ripe, and as those children sang, everything sweetly and comfortably slid into a new gift: "To some it is given by the Holy Ghost to know that Jesus Christ is the Son of God, and that he was crucified for the sins of the world." That testimony has never wavered. It has been strengthened while I've been moving my feet in service more than study. I have learned to always acknowledge the Lord's hand in all things. I trust Him.

Our homes must be a treasury of testimony. In that treasury, our children can discover their gifts too.

Parenting Self-Examination

1. How is your family prayer life? Any need for new patterns?
2. How is your library of learning standard? Need to make any new acquisitions? Does anything in the library need to be moved out?
3. How is your legacy of love? What can you do to improve it?
4. A treasury is a place where revenue or treasure is stored, managed, and cared for. Is testimony a prominent part of your treasury? Conduct an audit and strengthen the value.

Scriptures for Study

3 Nephi 18:21	Alma 37:36	D&C 46:11–14
D&C 88:118	Mosiah 4:15	Alma 13:28

A Parting Thought

President Monson challenged us, "My brothers and sisters, let us determine, whatever our circumstance, to make our houses happy homes. Let us open wide the windows of our hearts, that each family member may feel welcome and 'at home.' Let us open also the doors of our very souls, that the dear Christ may enter" ("Hallmark of a Happy Home," *Ensign*, October 2001).

Remember: No recipes. Study. Self-examine. Do your best. Live worthy of the Holy Ghost. Pray that the Lord will touch your doings and consecrate them for the blessing and benefit of you, your children, and your grandchildren.

Principle 22

When Things Don't Go as Planned

"When I left high school, my goals were to attend college for at least a couple of years, get married to a handsome man, and have four perfect, beautiful children (two boys and two girls). My husband was to have a large income so I wouldn't need to work, and then I planned to do Church and community service. Thankfully, one of my goals was to be an active and faithful member of the Church. Well, as you may know, many of my goals were not realized in the way I had hoped. I finished college, served a mission, got a job, continued on with my schooling to earn a master's degree, and continued working in my profession for many years. . . . Nothing had gone as I had planned except for one thing. I tried to be an active and faithful member of the Church. For this I am most grateful. It has made all the difference in my life." (Barbara Thompson, "Mind the Gap," *Ensign*, November 2009)

ISTER THOMPSON is one of many single women in the
Church who have never married or are in the ranks of the
divorced or widowed. This status also includes men. Many of
these brothers and sisters do not have children of their own while
others work to fulfill roles of provider and nurturer. Yes, these who
move forward in faith remain faithful contributors to the kingdom. Being close to some who are in this situation, I have listened
to their aching hearts about how difficult it is to sit in meetings
and hear sermons preached in a culture where marriage, family,
and two-parent homes are the standard. Unfortunately, some even
make the choice to retreat into inactivity. That choice comes with
a price.

Elder Boyd K. Packer taught, "Those who do not marry or
those who cannot have children are not excluded from the eternal
blessings they seek but which, for now, remain beyond their reach.
We do not always know how or when blessings will present themselves, but the promise of eternal increase will not be denied any
faithful individual who makes and keeps sacred covenants" ("The
Witness," *Ensign*, May 2014).

The key for these singles, parents or not, is to be faithful,
make and keep covenants, and move forward. To illustrate I will
share the story of one single sister with whom I became acquainted
in Latin America. But I am going to take a long way around to her
story. We had the privilege of working with her missionary son in
Chile. He was an extraordinary young man. From the moment I
met, him I could feel a special spirit. Most impressive to me was his
smile, respect, courtesy, and natural enthusiasm. I came to know
him in our regular monthly interviews. I went out and worked
with him, observing closely, and became more and more inspired
by his nature. In zone conferences, I noticed how he interacted
with other missionaries and was respected by them. When he had
about six months left, I felt impressed to call him to be my assistant. There he would get the opportunity to have a more significant influence on the missionaries across the mission and would

be especially helpful in our training of new missionaries coming into the field.

Assistants, because they work so closely with the president, come to understand both the blessings and the challenges of presiding over missionaries. They become aware that a small percentage of the missionaries can require a large percentage of the mission president's time and patience. One particular missionary was a challenge to his companions, ward leaders, and any North American he had contact with, including his president, and was selective in his obedience to standard mission rules. After consulting with the Area Presidency and the missionary's stake president several times, I was left to determine if and when to take action to send him home early.

A couple of weeks after my new assistant was called, the phone rang and a zone leader informed me our challenging missionary had again left his companion. I confess my disappointment quickly transformed into animated instruction to the secretary to purchase an airline ticket for the missionary—he was going home that day. The assistants were instructed then to find the missionary and tell him to pack his bags and prepare to return home. I tried to move to other important matters.

Sitting at my desk, I could see my assistant standing respectfully in the doorway. He politely asked to visit with me, and I invited him in. He closed the door, came to the side of my desk chair, and knelt before me, saying, "President, you can't send him home. Do you know what will happen to him if you send him home? He will get lost and become inactive. You are the president and will make the right decision, but please don't send him home." He paused for a brief moment and then said, "President, release me as assistant, even though I have just begun. I will be his companion. He can have another chance. Please don't send him home. I will be his companion. Elder ____ and I will leave now and go find him. That will give you a chance to pray about it. Okay?"

I didn't say so then, but I thought it was one of the craziest ideas I'd ever heard of. I wanted to say no. The assistants went to their task and I prayed. I fought the answer until my heart was softened. I did not want to release him, but the Lord did. A new companionship was formed. What we observed next was a miracle. The problem missionary began to change in every way imaginable. His dress, his countenance, and his smile were the most visible, but something was changing in his heart. In the next three months the transformation was complete, and the problem elder was trustworthy and ready to be given increased responsibility. Meanwhile, they were able to prepare a number of people for baptism.

Leaving out many sweet details, I was impressed to consider extending the former assistant's mission for a special assignment.

Now we are going to return to his mother's story. Extending a missionary's time of service is not an arbitrary decision. The Area Presidency and Missionary Department had to be consulted and permission had to be granted. A personal first step in the process was for me to consult his mother. I called her on the telephone and first engaged in some small talk, and then the conversation went something like this, "Sister, I'm wondering how you would feel if we were to extend your son's mission by six weeks?" I knew this was a single mother who needed her son. The pause continued for ten or more seconds, and then this valiant soul replied, "My son was born while I was single. I was baptized and became a member of the Church while I was pregnant. I prayed to Heavenly Father and told Him that my son was His son and that I would consecrate him to do whatever the Lord needed him for. I would not only give him to the Lord but also do all in my power to prepare him for service." She finished, "So, President Christensen, if the Lord needs him for six more weeks, or six more months, or even six more years, he is the Lord's. And whatever the Lord needs is fine with me." I understood better why this missionary was such an incredible man. His mother had committed herself and her son to the Lord. She stayed true and faithful all of her days as a single mother with one objective: to raise her son up unto the Lord so that he could be of service in the building of the kingdom.

In her quote, Sister Thompson states that not everything we plan in our lives turns out the way we had hoped. No one marries planning to get a divorce. Few singles plan to be alone. One hopes not to be left widowed. We are all subject to the agency of others and to situations beyond our control. But there are some things we can control, like our minds, our wills, and our commitments. We can give our lives to the Lord and His ways. We can commit to the Lord that we will do all in our power to prepare our children, even in a one-parent home, to be worthy servants and follow Him (remembering they also have their agency).

So, as singles, stay true and faithful and be fully engaged in the gospel and its covenants. The Lord gave the following promise through His servant:

> As a servant of the Lord, acting in the office to which I have been ordained, I give those in such circumstances a promise that there will be nothing essential to your salvation and exaltation that shall not in due time rest upon you. Arms now empty will be filled, and hearts now hurting from broken dreams and yearning will be healed. (Boyd K. Packer, "The Witness," *Ensign*, May 2014)

Parenting Self-Examination

1. How is your commitment level to the Lord and the building of His kingdom?
2. What can you do to step up your commitment to Him?
3. If you know some who are single and struggling with their testimonies of feeling estranged, what can you do to lift them up and help them to see their positive possibilities as a single?

Scriptures for Study

Proverbs 3:5–6	2 Nephi 4:34–35
2 Nephi 2:24	2 Nephi 9:20

A Parting Thought

I will part with the words of Elder David S. Baxter,

Whatever your circumstances or the reasons for them, how wonderful you are. Day to day you face the struggles of life, . . . doing it largely alone. . . . You run your household, watch over your family, sometimes struggle to make ends meet, and miraculously you even find the wherewithal to serve in the Church in significant ways. . . . While you cannot change the past, you can shape the future. Along the way you will obtain compensatory blessings, even if they are not immediately apparent. ("Faith, Fortitude, Fulfillment: A Message to Single Parents," *Ensign*, May 2012)

Remember: No recipes. Study. Self-examine. Do your best. Live worthy of the Holy Ghost. Pray that the Lord will touch your doings and consecrate them for the blessing and benefit of you, your children, and your grandchildren.

Principle 23

Do It the Lord's Way!

"To set our house in an order pleasing to the Lord, we need to do it His way. . . . Each father should remember that 'no power or influence can or ought to be maintained by virtue of the priesthood, only by persuasion, by long-suffering, by gentleness and meekness, and by love unfeigned.' Parents are to be living examples of 'kindness, and pure knowledge, which . . . greatly enlarge the soul.' Each mother and father should lay aside selfish interests and avoid any thought of hypocrisy, physical force, or evil speaking. Parents soon learn that each child has an inborn yearning to be free. Each individual wants to make his or her own way. No one wants to be restrained, even by a well-intentioned parent. But all of us can cling to the Lord." (Russell M. Nelson, " 'Set in Order Thy House,' " *Ensign*, November 2001)

So WHAT's the little plaque on your desk, President?" asked one of my counselors. " 'Do It the Lord's Way!' Is there a story behind it?"

There is a story. We had just purchased our first starter home and were moving in. The doorbell rang and there stood a man in his early sixties with a big smile. "I'm Bishop Jones, and I came to help you move in. We've been expecting you, Brother and Sister Christensen," he said cheerfully. We didn't have a lot of stuff to unload at that simple time of our lives, so with the help of others, it didn't take long. We visited for a few minutes and Bishop Jones asked me to come to his office the next day.

When I arrived the next morning at the appointed time, I saw a wooden plaque with a gold engraved plate sitting on his bare desktop that read, "Do It the Lord's Way!" He asked me a few questions and issued me a call to serve as the Young Men president in the Mesa 29th Ward. I accepted, and he asked what experiences I had as a youth in the Young Men's program. I shared a few of the positive things I had experienced growing up. "Well," he said, "I'm officially going to ask you to forget everything you know or remember from your experience as a youth or anything you think you know about it now. Just forget it!" He stated this with some emphasis. Then he opened his desk drawer and pulled out a manual of instruction for Young Men leaders. He looked me straight in the eyes and invited me to read it from cover to cover, mark it up, and take notes. Gently pointing to the plaque on the top of his desk, he said, "Brother Christensen, let's have a Young Men's program doing it the Lord's way." That left such a profound impression on me that twelve years later when I was called as a bishop, I shared it with our new bishopric. My executive secretary, Brother Rasmussen, gave me my own plaque as a gift. Since that time I have had it on my desk or displayed prominently in my offices. I have a second that reads "Hagalo a la Manera del Señor" for the days of serving in beloved Latin America. And it has served as a steady reminder in everything I have done, taught, and experienced.

In a responsibility so important and vital as parenting, I join my witness with Elder Nelson's counsel that "to set our house in an order pleasing to the Lord, we need to do it His way" (Russell M. Nelson, "'Set in Order Thy House," *Ensign*, November 2001).

His way is identified by the scriptural passages in Doctrine and Covenants 121:41–42. Let's break down the verses and study the words he uses to describe His way. To fathers, He said in verse 41:

- "No power or influence"—*influence* is a word for leadership or guidance.
- "can or ought to be maintained"—*maintained* means to conserve, preserve, or keep alive.
- "by virtue of the priesthood"—*virtue* means goodness, purity, and righteousness.
- "only by persuasion"—*persuasion* means to coax, urge, and convince.
- "by long-suffering"—*long-suffering* means to be patient, tolerant, and forgiving.
- "by gentleness"—to be gentle is to be tender, considerate, understanding, compassionate, sweet-tempered, and good natured.
- "and meekness"—to be meek is to be yielding, humble, and mild.
- "and by love unfeigned"—*love* means to care, have goodwill, and tenderness. *Unfeigned* means sincere, real, honest, heartfelt, and unforced.

In summary, the Lord expects a father to be a leader and guide who keeps alive goodness and purity while urging his children to do good. He coaxes and seeks to convince his children with patience and understanding. He is forgiving and sweet-tempered about his efforts to get his children to do what they ought to do. He is humble and yielding. He understands he is not perfect. He is honest with his children and knows that to force compliance is in Satan's realm. He is tender and mild.

Verse 42 states that parents are to operate in their roles with:

- "kindness"—*kind* means to be warm, loving, and thoughtful.
- "pure knowledge"—*pure* means to be honorable, ethical, and honest. *Knowledge* means wisdom and awareness.

We are to be warm, loving, and thoughtful when dealing with our children and to treat them honorably with wisdom and awareness. Elder Nelson reminds us that parents need to:

- "lay aside selfish interests"—*selfish* means self-absorbed or egocentric.
- "avoid any thought of hypocrisy"—*thought* means views, feelings, and conclusions. *Hypocrisy* means duplicity or two-faced, deceitful, or fraud.
- "[avoid] physical force"—meaning bodily or corporeal.
- "[avoid] evil speaking"—means to communicate in a foul, harmful, vile, or shocking way. (Russell M. Nelson, "Set in Order Thy House," *Ensign*, November 2001)

Therefore, parents are to avoid being overly concerned with themselves and how children affect or impact them. They ought to balance their roles of nurturing their children with the concern for themselves. They should not use emotional or physical force to coerce, intimidate, or bully their children. Communicating in foul or harmful ways is not the Lord's way.

Parenting Self-Examination

1. In our word study and corresponding self-examination, define just one or two things you want to focus on to improve. Choose just one or two for now; you can pick another later.
2. Of all the characteristics of the Lord's way, can you see attributes with which you feel you've done pretty well? Write them down and remember them. Congratulations. Keep it up.

Scriptures for Study

| D&C 121:41–42 | John 14:15 | Matthew 19:17 |
| Abraham 3:24–26 | Alma 41:10 | |

A Parting Thought

I feel confident that no mother or father has ever been perfect in parenting the Lord's way. It is easy to remember our own violations of that principle. Mothers struggle daily in their attempt to execute their nurturing role without making a mistake. All of us as parents fall short. However, the Lord is good to us and defines a standard we can continually try to reach. As we do so, we will be inspired and be guided in our parenting. Incidentally, when your children grow up, some of the best, most humorous, rolling-in-laughter stories told in family circles will come from those less-than-perfect moments. I'm confident that He will consecrate our best efforts and strivings to the good of our children. The secret is to keep trying.

Remember: No recipes. Study. Self-examine. Do your best. Live worthy of the Holy Ghost. Pray that the Lord will touch your doings and consecrate them for the blessing and benefit of you, your children, and your grandchildren.

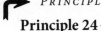

Principle 24

Creating Family Cultures

"Let me suggest five things parents can do to create stronger family cultures: First, parents can pray in earnest, asking our Eternal Father to help love, understand, and guide the children He has sent them. Second, they can hold family prayer, scripture study, and family home evenings and eat together. . . . Third, parents can fully avail themselves of the Church's support network. . . . Fourth, parents share their testimonies often with their children. . . . Fifth, we can organize our families based on clear, simple family rules and expectations, wholesome family traditions and rituals, and 'family economics,' where children have household responsibilities and can earn allowances so that they can learn to budget, save, and pay tithing on the money they earn." (L. Tom Perry, "Becoming Goodly Parents," *Ensign*, November 2012)

A CULTURE IS defined as the customs, attitudes, and behaviors of a particular social group. Businesses go to great lengths to consider and establish a culture that defines who the company is and how it operates. There is a distinct culture in recreational groups such as skateboarders, fisherman, professional sports players, and so on. Sub-cultures emerge among motorcycle enthusiasts, truckers, followers of rodeo and so on. There is a definite Latter-day Saint culture, and for good or bad, there are sub-cultures in it. Cultures can be planned and molded, or they just happen. A culture is at the foundation of the way we operate and think. Elder Perry provides five excellent principles to help us develop a family culture that, if embraced and lived, can produce excellent results in our family.

First, make a conscious and consistent effort to align ourselves with Heavenly Father, who is the spiritual parent of the children who come to our homes. He knew them before we did. He loves them. He desires to help. My parents got married rather young. They were not prepared to be parents in most ways, but from their first days of parenting, they were so humbly aware of their inadequacies that they engaged the Lord in every effort. In later years, they were often sought out about their parenting skills in raising nine children. Their answer was always the same: "We raised our family on our knees." Heavenly Father wants the best for His children. Keep Him in the forefront of helping us know how to operate day by day.

Second, fully engage in family prayer, scripture study, family home evening, and eating together. The culture in the home of my youth was kneeling in family prayer twice each day at the breakfast and dinner table. "We never miss a meal," Dad said, "so if we pray as a family at breakfast and dinner, we won't miss our family prayer either." In our family culture, we came to the table and knelt by our chairs, indicating we were there and ready. Dad called on one of us to be the voice. Mom held the record for the longest prayers. And of course, the youngest gave short prayers that made the older children snicker.

I believe the standard of family prayer, scripture study, and family home evening has improved (notice I did not say "been perfected") over the years. Interestingly, the standard of eating together has seemed to become more challenging. Be aware of the prophetic counsel and do your best to follow.

Third, Elder Perry suggests we take full advantage of the support programs of the Church, remembering that the programs of the Church are to support the family. While we are responsible for teaching our children, the Church has an extraordinary safety and support net. A plethora of wonderful Primary teachers set a wonderful foundation for my children. Scouting with men like Brothers Thornock, Shapiro, Reed, Nygren, and Willis were great blessings to me in raising my sons. The Young Women program with its values and extraordinary advisors blessed my daughters then and enhances their capacity to serve now. Seminary teachers reached my children with certain principles that they didn't seem ready for with me. The list goes on and on. The organization and programs of the Church helped my wife and I in our effort to raise good children. In added measure Gospel Doctrine, Relief Society, and priesthood lessons energized us with capacity to keep on. The *Ensign*, *New Era*, and *Friend* are blessings and resources, especially the general conference issues.

Fourth, bear your testimony. Our lives are our testimony. *Preach My Gospel* states, "Your testimony may be as simple as 'Jesus Christ is the Son of God' or 'I have learned for myself that the Book of Mormon is true'" (*Preach My Gospel: A Guide to Missionary Service* [Salt Lake City: The Church of Jesus Christ of Latter-day Saints, 2004], 198–99). We can all get better at sharing our testimony in short, simple statements in our normal chats and family discussion. As we listen to our kids tell us of something that happened at school, we can say, "Wow, that shows me that Heavenly Father loves you and all of us," or, "I've learned that the story of the good Samaritan really does apply to us, and you showed that compassion in the way you handled that situation," or, "Jesus really did show us the way to act in that situation." Others statements like, "Didn't Heavenly Father make a beautiful world?" or, "I'm grateful we can repent and try to do better," or, "Heavenly Father made our bodies to repair and heal. That's a miracle" are testimony statements.

Fifth, "organize [your] families based on clear, simple family rules and expectations, wholesome family traditions, and rituals, and 'family economics,' where children have household responsibilities and can earn allowances so that they can learn to budget, save, and pay tithing on the money they earn" (L. Tom Perry, "Becoming Goodly Parents," *Ensign*, November 2012). It seems that an organization based on principles more than rules is preferred. When laws and rules are written, then enforcement is incumbent. Once the law is established, then you have to police and judge. Elder Perry's suggestion is inspired—clear, simple, and defined expectations. For our children, the hour to be home on weekends was midnight. They may not have always liked it, but it was easy to understand, and they knew it was expected. Parents can work on establishing principles and a few rules with the help of the Holy Ghost. Simplicity, clarity, and consistency are all key.

Traditions and rituals are my favorite culture-builders. Sometimes they are born in spontaneity, and other times they are planned. In the early spring of 1979, my wife and I had discussed our philosophy about the Easter Bunny versus the Resurrection of the Savior. We knew where we wanted our emphasis to be. We got busy and didn't think much about it.

Late on "Easter Eve," I knew I didn't have much more time. As I pondered in bed, an idea came to my mind. I am an early riser and knew the projected time for the sun to rise. A half hour before sunrise, I "kidnapped" our five small children from their beds and escorted them and their mother to the trampoline in our backyard. With pillows and blankets, we lay listening to the birds and sounds of the early Easter morning. A few minutes before the sun peeked its head over the Superstition Mountains and shown its light on us, I told the story of the first Easter morning and the Resurrection. A tradition was born! Three decades later, the tradition continues with our children's children. In cold country, the trampoline is replaced with a suburban driving to a hill facing the east or overlooking a temple. That and many other rituals and traditions have laced our family culture with meaning and substance, as well as laughter and fun.

Teaching important economic principles are critical in the culture. We found ways to help our children earn money but decided that chores were just a part of being a family and helping out. Rotating family chores were not compensated with money but with tangible satisfaction in making a trip to the Dairy Queen or a favorite yogurt shop. Extra jobs, not on the chore chart, merited earning money and subsequently helped us teach the law of tithing. One summer of working for Dad on his to-do list caused our son to resolve to get a real job that was not so demanding. The Holy Ghost will help you figure out what's best for you and your family.

Parenting Self-Examination

1. Do you fully engage Heavenly Father in your quest to establish, maintain, or maybe tweak your family culture? What can you do to improve your relationship with Him?
2. What can you do to improve the basics of family prayer, scripture study, family home evening, and eating dinner together?
3. How can you use Church programs to strengthen your family?
4. Conduct an audit of the family rules. Are they simple? Clear? Require too much policing and supervision? What can you do to improve them?
5. What traditions have you established? Can you think of new ways to solidify the culture you desire?
6. Is your family economic philosophy what you want it to be? How does it influence your culture? Is tithing integrated and taught at an early age? What needs fixing or minor tweaking?

Scriptures for Study

| Proverbs 22:6 | Psalm 127:3 (1–5) | D&C 93:40 |
| Mosiah 5:15 | 3 Nephi 6:14 | |

A Parting Thought

Considering family culture is one of the most enjoyable things we do. What meaningful traditions from your family do you want to carry on together? Keep things simple. Add, eliminate, or adjust as you feel prompted. Cultures emerge and can be a glue for the family. We need to make sure they are moving us toward the Savior.

Remember: No recipes. Study. Self-examine. Do your best. Live worthy of the Holy Ghost. Pray that the Lord will touch your doings and consecrate them for the blessing and benefit of you, your children, and your grandchildren.

Principle 25

The Enduring Influence of Grandparents

"Grandparents can have a profound influence on their grand-children. Their time is generally not as encumbered and busy as the parents', so books can be opened and read, stories can be told, and application of gospel principles can be taught. Children then obtain a perspective of life which not only is rewarding but can bring them security, peace, and strength." (Ezra Taft Benson, *Teaching of the Presidents of the Church: Ezra Taft Benson* [Salt Lake City: The Church of Jesus Christ of Latter-day Saints, 2014], 203–16)

WHILE STUDYING to write this chapter, I found that there are many studies that support the fact that grandparents can play a tremendous role in the positive upbringing of grandchildren. From Oxford University to BYU, there are many studies and investigations that show that grandparents from all backgrounds can serve an important role that contributes to their grandchildren's well-being. They help their grandchildren solve problems they may be experiencing, especially in talking with them about plans for their future.

Principal Investigator Professor Ann Buchanan, director of the Centre for Research into Parenting and Children in the Department of Social Policy and Social Work at Oxford University said,

We were surprised by the huge amount of informal caring that the grandparents were doing and how in some cases they were filling the parenting gap for hard working parents. Most adolescents really welcomed this relationship. What was especially interesting was the links we found between involved grandparents and adolescent well-being. Closeness was not enough: only grandparents who got stuck in and did things with their grandchildren had this positive impact on them. ("Involved Grandparents Significantly Associated with Better-Adjusted Grandchildren," *University of Oxford Newsletter*, June 2008)

The studies showed that grandparents, even from biblical times when the family was more than a parent and child unit, provided insight. The family then included all who were related by blood and marriage. The old were respected for their wisdom and life experience. Other cultures honored the elders or elderly as those who gave direction and counsel to their families. Grandpas and grandmas can help their grandchildren form values, ideals, and beliefs. The older generation can have a strong impact on their grandchildren's sense of identity, influence their religious development in major ways, and help them discover meaningful career paths. Studies show that grandmas play an especially important role in the development their grandchildren's values. And grandpas and grandmas equally influence the development of work ethics. Another role is being the "family historians" who serve as a link between past generations and future direction. Helping children become attached to and taught by the humanness of the past can help them have a much better time dealing with the future.

My mother was preserved for several years after my dad passed. It was a great blessing to see how she continued to influence grandchildren who came to clean her home or help her get to Church meetings. She was pivotal in helping granddaughters and grandsons who were confused for short seasons of their lives. She was affirming, positive, and loving. I also noted that she was the one who kept us all connected, even from long distances. She spent the last years of her life creating dozens of three-ring notebooks with collections of stories and photographs for each of her children and grandchildren. These collections have served as reminders of her love and support to us, when she was with us and now that she's on the other side of the veil. Her encouragement and endorsing love extended to young mothers in the family helped them do their best and carry on with faith in the future. Every child in the extended family felt remembered and valued by my mother, who was affectionately called "GG." Her influence continues as we remember and revere her.

Grandparents serve as mentors, teachers, nurturers, and even playmates. From academia, we can learn much that substantiates the counsel given by our prophets, apostles, and other leaders. President Gordon B. Hinckley, speaking to the mature women of the Church, once said,

> Now to you grandmothers and great-grandmothers may I just say a word. Tremendous has been your experience. Tremendous is your understanding. You can be as an anchor in a world of shifting values. You have lived long, buffed and polished by the adversities of life through which you have passed. Quiet are your ways, deliberate your counsel. You dearly beloved women are such treasures in this topsy-turvy society. ("Stand Strong against the Wiles of the World," *Ensign*, November 1995)

I have seen a wise grandmother sit with her grandchildren and show them a way to study their patriarchal blessings. She reminded her grandchildren that interpretation of blessings is left to them as guided by the Spirit or in some cases counseling with the patriarch who gave the blessing. She showed her grandchildren how to study their blessing from a different perspective. She took a piece of paper and drew a line down the middle and one across the top of the sheet. She then labeled the left-hand column "Promised Blessings" and the right-hand column "Counsel." As they read the blessings together, she asked over and over again, "Is that statement a promise or blessing, or is it counsel to you to do something?" She acted only as facilitator. When completed, the grandchildren had a new way of remembering the things the Lord tells them to do so that they may be worthy of receiving the promised blessings. Those grandchildren looked at their grandmother with adoring eyes, gave her a hug, and expressed their love for her. Each were blessed.

In the Guatemala MTC, I once noticed a particular missionary who had a booklet sitting by *Preach My Gospel* that he referred to when I was facilitating a discussion on the Apostasy and Restoration. While it wasn't his nature to dominate any discussion we had held previously, this particular day he was quite active in his participation. I soon noticed that he and his companion were both looking at the aforementioned little spiral-bound notebook and both sharing correct and meaningful answers to members of their zone. After the discussion concluded, I approached him and his companion to comment about how impressed I was with their answers and see where they were coming from. Generally, missionaries are encouraged not to have any materials outside of the Missionary Department-approved library, so I thought it well to see if I needed to give any encouragement toward that counsel. After I applauded their answers and insight, I asked if I could see the little booklet. It was quiet for a few seconds as I flipped through the little homemade spiral bound book. Then this elder broke the silence with quiet confidence as he said, "I got it from our family MTC. My grandpa holds an MTC for all his grandchildren who will be going on a mission in the next year." *Wow*, I thought, *a grandpa MTC*. I'll bet those missionaries in that family have a sense of belonging, of pure desire to be obedient servants.

A student once told me that her grandparents gave her a Book of Mormon study journal. They taught her how to read passages of scripture and write her impressions about what that passage meant to her and how she should apply that to living her life. I sensed she had come to know how to study scripture with the capacity of transferring it to application in her life.

It was interesting to me how President Faust counseled mission presidents when we were at the seminar for new mission presidents. In his wisdom and the power of his stewardship, he said something like this, "Now presidents, you are going to develop very strong relationships with most of your missionaries. It will be almost like father and son relationships. You may even be inclined to refer to them like Helaman referred to the stripling warriors when he said, 'And I did join my two thousand sons, (for they are worthy to be called sons)' (Alma 56:10). I think if I could give you counsel, treat them more like grandsons than sons. Your relationship and influence will be better with them if you maintain a grandfather-grandson relationship." He went on to say how many times fathers are a little quicker to correct than grandfathers, how sometimes the closeness of the relationship with fathers and sons tended to have more correction than affirmation. "I just think you'll accomplish more having a more grandfatherly, patient relationship than a father-son relationship," he concluded.

Now to grandchildren these grandparents and the children of these parents, the day may come when they feel unused and that their life experience doesn't matter much to the others in the workplace or in the community. That can be a hard time in the lives of the elderly.

Take care that doesn't happen in the family circle. With my own father, from the time I was a newlywed to the day Dad passed at nearly the age of ninety, we had a weekly telephone call and conversation. It mostly centered around the weather, our gardens, and how the family was doing. One day, my son Aaron called Dad and asked him for some advice regarding planting his garden. He knew my dad's version of a home garden was a half acre showpiece that provided fresh seasonal vegetables for all who would come and help themselves. Aaron had called him for advice and Dad shared his knowledge. Now, in our weekly telephone conversations, what new topic surfaced in our interchange? "How's Aaron's garden?" I learned to ask Aaron the same question in our conversations, so I knew how to respond to my dad. That interest and request for counsel enhanced the life of my dad, linked our three generations, and blessed us all.

Parenting Self-Examination

1. If you are a grandparent, were there any nudges to your heart when reading this chapter? What are you going to do to respond to stirrings? Write them down and take action.
2. If you are a parent, how can you encourage and facilitate better child-grandparent relationships?
3. If you have a living grandparent, then your children have great-grandparents. What can you do to engage and exhibit interest and care for you grandparents? How can you help your children get to know and love their great-grandparents?

Scriptures for Study

Proverbs 17:6	Proverbs 13:22	Psalm 145:4
Psalm 103:17	Genesis 48:9	Titus 2:1–5

A Parting Thought

Sometimes grandparents may not have the same set of values you have or want your children to embrace. Consult the Lord relative to the matter. Draw thick lines where you need to and be sure to teach your children about filtering messages that may be given by grandparents who either never had testimonies or have forgotten them. In all of it, be sure to show honor and respect. One day you will be grandparents, so be the model of how to honor and treat grandparents. You will be guided by the Holy Ghost how to best handle this.

Remember: No recipes. Study. Self-examine. Do your best. Live worthy of the Holy Ghost. Pray that the Lord will touch your doings and consecrate them for the blessing and benefit of you, your children, and your grandchildren.

Principle 26

Rescue in Love

"If someone in your family is wandering in strange paths, you are a rescuer, engaged in the greatest rescue effort the Church has ever known. I testify from personal experience: There is no failure except in giving up. It is never too early or too late to begin. Do not worry about what has happened in the past. Pick up the phone. Write a note. Make a visit. Extend the invitation to come home. Don't be afraid or embarrassed. Your child is Heavenly Father's child. You are about His work. He has promised to gather His children, and He is with you." (Robert D. Hales, "Our Duty to God: The Mission of Parents and Leaders to the Rising Generation," *Ensign*, May 2010)

I'M FAIRLY certain all of us love people who have lost their grip on the rod of iron, made bad choices, and are wandering in strange roads (see 1 Nephi 8:32). It's heartbreaking to watch. It's as though their eyes are wide open, but they are unable to see. Or worse, those who know they are self-destructing but don't have the desire or willpower to make necessary course corrections.

In those instances, it is important to remember that, while there are many things we can do to help them, the things that will change their courses can only be done by the Lord, in His way. We cannot force change, and we must not negate agency.

In the celestial room of the temple, I was present when a

brokenhearted mother sobbed uncontrollably, knowing that one of her children was not present. The day was a special occasion, the first such event in her family when all could have been with her in the house of the Lord. Because of shortsighted choices and an unrepentant heart, her child—who had participated many times before—was unable to enter on that special day.

I have observed a good and righteous father who helplessly looked on as his son took sporadic steps toward making eternal covenants and commitments he would not likely keep. Hopeful that his son was moving in the right direction, his fear discounted his joy. A casual attitude and flippant approach to things eternal concerned his father, who knew that the Lord is "not to be mocked" (D&C 63:58).

I knew a mother whose life was emerging from a past of drugs, illicit sex, and abuse. Her own life was on the mend, but she watched as her children began to make the same choices she made twenty-five years ago that took her through a mire of muck and sadness. She wondered, "What can I do? How can I make my own new start a blessing in my children's lives, though they literally stand on the brink of a future like my own?"

We could go on. You can, no doubt, add examples as well. So what can be done?

Elder Richard G. Scott provides seven ways of parenting for us to consider (see "To Help a Loved One in Need," *Ensign*, May 1988). Other prophets share their perspectives in each of the guidelines.

1. "Love without limitations."

Never withdraw love for children or family members who struggle.

> We must never out of anger, lock the door of our home or our heart to our children. Like the prodigal son, our children need to know that when they come to themselves they can turn to us for love and counsel. (Robert D Hales, "Strengthening Families: Our Sacred Duty," *Ensign*, May 1999)

In his conference talk on tolerance and love, Elder Russell M. Nelson taught, "Real love for the sinner may compel courageous confrontation—not acquiescence! Real love does not support self-destructing behavior" ("'Teach Us Tolerance and Love,'" *Ensign*, May 1994, 71).

Parents should also remember the Lord's frequent teaching: "Verily, thus saith the Lord unto you whom I love, and whom I love I also chasten that their sins may be forgiven, for with the chastisement I prepare a way for their deliverance in all things out of temptation, and I have loved you" (D&C 95:1).

2. "Do not condone the transgressions, but extend every hope and support to the transgressor."

> Parents may wonder how to be generally supportive of their young adult without condoning specific immoral behavior. Harsh and judgmental reactions, threats to disown them, or other mistreatment of such a son or daughter do not help. Parents need to continue to extend loving concern to the young man or woman while upholding God's law of chastity and morality. (John K. Carmack, "When Our Children Go Astray," *Ensign*, February 1997)

3. "Teach truth."

We must understand that true doctrine will change behavior more effectively than trying to convince people they are sinning. As we facilitate discussion, we must involve the real teacher, the Holy Ghost. The Lord said, "To preach my gospel by the Spirit, even the Comforter which was sent forth to teach the truth" (D&C 50:14).

Elder Boyd K. Packer taught, "The study of the doctrines of the gospel will improve behavior quicker than a study of behavior will improve behavior. Preoccupation with unworthy behavior can lead to unworthy behavior. That is why we stress so forcefully the study of the doctrines of the gospel" ("Little Children," *Ensign*, November 1986).

We will do well to teach them the truth relative to the Savior: "And we talk of Christ, we rejoice in Christ, we preach of Christ, we prophesy of Christ, and we write according to our prophecies, that our children may know to what source they may look for a remission of their sins" (2 Nephi 25:26).

4. "Honestly forgive as often as is required."

Nephi forgave his brothers Laman and Lemuel many times: "And it came to pass that I did frankly forgive them all that they had done" (1 Nephi 7:21).

We have no record of Lehi and Sariah's response, but we can imagine their hearts were filled with hope and love. They likely taught forgiveness and mercy as they dealt with the dynamics of others in the family circle.

The Lord admonishes and reminds us, "I, the Lord, will forgive whom I will forgive, but of you it is required to forgive all men" (D&C 64:10).

"Then came Peter to him, and said, Lord, how oft shall my brother sin against me, and I forgive him? till seven times? Jesus saith unto him, I say not unto thee, Until seven times: but, Until seventy times seven" (Matthew 18:21–22).

5. "Pray trustingly."

Let the father and mother, who are members of this Church and Kingdom, take a righteous course, and strive with all their might never to do a wrong, but to do good all their lives; if they have one child or one hundred children, if they conduct themselves towards them as they should, binding them to the Lord by their faith and prayers, I care not where those children go, they are bound up to their parents by an everlasting tie, and no power of earth or hell can separate them from their parents in eternity; they will return again to the fountain from whence they sprang. (Brigham Young, *Teachings of Presidents of the Church: Brigham Young* [Salt Lake City: The Church of Jesus Christ of Latter-day Saints, 1997], 163)

6. *"Keep perspective."*

When I take a small pebble and place it directly in front of my eye, it takes on the appearance of a mighty boulder. It is all I can see. It becomes all-consuming—like the problems of a loved one that affect our lives every waking moment. When the things you realistically can do to help are done, leave the matter in the hands of the Lord and worry no more. Do not feel guilty because you cannot do more. Do not waste your energy on useless worry. The Lord will take the pebble that fills your vision and cast it down among the challenges you will face in your eternal progress. It will then be seen in perspective. In time, you will feel impressions and know how to give further help. (Richard G. Scott, "To Help a Loved One in Need," *Ensign*, May 1988)

7. *"Never give up on a loved one, never!"*

Let's consider again Elder Hales's perspective as taught in the opening of this chapter:

If someone in your family is wandering in strange paths, you are a rescuer, engaged in the greatest rescue effort the Church has ever known. I testify from personal experience: There is no failure except in giving up. It is never too early or too late to begin. Do not worry about what has happened in the past. Pick up the phone. Write a note. Make a visit. Extend an invitation to come home. Don't be afraid or embarrassed. Your child is Heavenly Father's child. You are about His work. He has promised to gather His children, and He is with you. ("Our Duty to God: The Mission of Parents and Leaders to the Rising Generation," *Ensign*, May 2010)

Besides yearning for the child who wanders, many parents perhaps come to the questions, "What did we do wrong?" Or, "Was this our fault?" Or, "Have we failed in our most important role in life?" President James E. Faust taught,

Who are good parents? They are those who have loving,

prayerfully, and earnestly tried to teach their children by example and precept "to pray, and to walk uprightly before the Lord." This is true even though some of their children are disobedient or worldly. Children come into this world with their own distinct spirits and personality traits. Some children "would challenge any set of parents under any set of circumstances. . . . Perhaps there are others who would bless the lives of, and be a joy to, almost any father or mother." Successful parents are those who have sacrificed and struggled to do the best they can in their own family circumstances. ("Dear Are the Sheep That Have Wandered," *Ensign*, May 2003)

Parenting Self-Examination

1. If you are struggling with a child or grandchild who is venturing in strange roads, which of these suggestions seems most helpful? Why?
2. If you know someone who is struggling with a child or grandchild, how can you help to bring a new perspective of hope?
3. Whether or not you have a family member who needs help, who can you reach out to and seek to rescue?

Scriptures for Study

D&C 50:14	Alma 42:31	Mormon 3:11; 5:1
D&C 63:58	D&C 95:1	D&C 25:26
1 Nephi 7:21	Matthew 18:21–22	

A Parting Thought

Parenting is a challenge. We should be careful not to become too proud or inclined toward arrogance if it is our blessing to have obedient and respectful children. President Faust suggests that children come to earth with predispositions for which we can take no credit nor fault. To those who have experienced heartbreak and have done their best to be righteous, diligent, prayerful, and faithful in parental responsibilities: refrain from heaping guilt upon yourselves for the way your children exercise their agency. I am grateful for the opportunity to share parenting with Heavenly Father. He loves all of His children and is watching over them and us. He knows of our humility and sorrow and will reward us for our engagement in His work to bring to pass the immortality and eternal life of His children. Be thankful and full of hope.

Remember: No recipes. Study. Self-examine. Do your best. Live worthy of the Holy Ghost. Pray that the Lord will touch your doings and consecrate them for the blessing and benefit of you, your children, and your grandchildren.

Principle 27

Joy in the Journey

"Day by day, minute by minute, second by second we went from where we were to where we are now. . . . Time never stands still; it must steadily march on, and with the marching come the changes. This is our one and only chance at mortal life—here and now. . . . Opportunities come, and then they are gone. I believe that among the greatest lessons we are to learn . . . are lessons that help us distinguish between what is important and what is not. I plead with you not to let those most important things pass you by as you plan for that illusive and nonexistent future when you will have time to do all that you want to do. . . . Let us relish life as we live it, find joy in the journey, and share our love with friends and family. One day each of us will run out of tomorrows." (Thomas S. Monson, "Finding Joy in the Journey," *Ensign*, November 2008)

PRINCIPLE 27

SOME DAYS, the journey of parenting can seem like an eternity. At other times, it is as aging Jacob described in the Book of Mormon: "Our lives passed away like as it were unto us a dream" (Jacob 7:26).

It seems only yesterday I was newly wed, living in Provo in basic housing, and working three jobs while my wife and I finished our final year at BYU. Graduation brought not only diplomas but also our first baby girl, Chantel. Reflecting back on those days seems to shrink time. I blink my eyes once and we are bringing our second little bundle, Creshel, to our new starter home in Mesa, Arizona. Blink again and we joyed in our third, Aaron, and fourth, Chalonn, who filled our family circle in Utah. A few more blinks and we're at eight children with Chelise, Chenae, Candra, and Devin in full gear in Arizona!

However, I begin to blend into those 10,600 days—basketball camps; tumbling lessons; soccer practice; cabin getaways; swimming; vacations; nearly a dozen relocations; over 1,500 family home evenings; nearly 22,000 family prayers and half as many scripture studies; thousands of bedtime stories; who knows the number of diaper changes, sibling squabbles, and noses that needed wiping; new drivers, dented fenders, teenage jobs, dating and late nights; school choir programs, ward talent shows; high adventure trips, Scout camps, girls' camps, Church callings; and of course jobs, business successes and failures, lane changes, and additional graduate degrees.

When I think of all that filled those years, I can understand why many young couples ask, "Does this merry-go-round (or sometimes "not-so-merry-go-round") ever end?" It can be exhausting!

President Monson taught, "If you are still in the process of raising children, be aware that the tiny fingerprints that show up on almost every newly cleaned surface, the toys scattered about the house, the piles and piles of laundry to be tackled will disappear all too soon and that you will—to your surprise—miss them profoundly."

He also states,

> If you have children who are grown and gone, in all likelihood
> you have occasionally felt pangs of loss and the recognition that
> you didn't appreciate that time of life as much as you should
> have. Of course, there is no going back, but only forward.
> Rather than dwelling on the past, we should make the most of
> today, of the here and now, doing all we can to provide pleasant
> memories for the future. ("Finding Joy in the Journey," *Ensign*,
> November 2008)

As busy and emotionally and physically draining as it was, I'm
so glad that those memories also include early morning walks and
talks with my sweetheart, trampoline-bed star gazing, hours of
hoop shooting, and thousands of ice-cream cones. I'm glad I don't
have many regrets—but there are a few. I think if I had those years
back and could do them over, I'd hope to do as Diana Loomans
wrote:

If I had my child to raise over again,
I'd finger paint more, and point the finger less.
I'd do less correcting, and more connecting.
I'd take my eyes off my watch, and watch with my eyes.
I would care to know less, and know to care more.
I'd take more hikes and fly more kites.
I'd stop playing serious, and seriously play.
I'd run through more fields, and gaze at more stars.
I'd do more hugging, and less tugging.
I would be firm less often, and affirm much more.
I'd build self-esteem first, and the house later.
I'd teach less about the love of power,
And more about the power of love
It matters not whether my child is big or small,
From this day forth, I'll cherish it all.
("If I Had My Child to Raise Over Again," dianaloomans.com;
used with permission)

Someone once impressed upon my mind that I need to *be where I am*. In other words:

When you are parents of little ones—enjoy it, savor it, be glad for it. It will be gone sooner than you think. Build memories where you are!

- When you are parents of teens—enjoy them, play, laugh, and remember that those days will also soon pass.
- When you are parents of missionaries or young adults in college, in military service, or courting—breathe it in and find joy in it.
- When you are parents of adult children, when you are grandparents with your faces to the sunset years—love it!

"Joy in the journey" is the perfect way to say it. Be where you are on the path and live it. No regrets!

Parenting Self-Examination

1. Take a look at the last five years of your life. What have been the highlights? Any tinges of regret? What can you do to change the results for the next five years? What will you do today?
2. In the spirit of being where you are and avoiding the "greener pasture" syndrome, what is the beauty of this moment on your path to tomorrow?
3. What do you want your children to remember about the "today chapter" of your life?

Scriptures for Study

Jacob 7:26	1 Thessalonians 5:18	1 Nephi 11:16–17
D&C 5:35	D&C 101:32–33	James 1:2–3
Romans 15:13		

A Parting Thought

When we think about the past, whether it includes mostly

sunshine and good times or rain clouds and mud, we would do well to adopt a personal philosophy: "The past is but ashes. Show me what you are doing today." If the past is something to brag about, remember it, but build something beautiful today. If the past is something you'd rather forget, learn from it and *do* forget the rest. Be where you are and make today great.

Remember: No recipes. Study. Self-examine. Do your best. Live worthy of the Holy Ghost. Pray that the Lord will touch your doings and consecrate them for the blessing and benefit of you, your children, and your grandchildren.

Principle 28

His Grace Sustains

"All of us face different family circumstances and home situations. All of us need strength in dealing with them. This strength comes from faith in the Savior's love and in the power of his Atonement. If we trustingly put our hand in the Savior's, we can claim the promise of the sacramental prayer to always have his Spirit with us. All problems are manageable with that strength, and all other problems are secondary in urgency to maintaining a strong spiritual life. . . . Strengthen yourselves by seeking the source of true strength—the Savior. Come unto him. He loves you. He desires your happiness. . . . Make him your strength, your daily companion, your rod and your staff. Let him comfort you. There is no burden we need bear alone. His grace compensates for our deficiencies. (Chieko N. Okazaki, "Strength in the Savior," *Ensign*, November 1993)

PARENTING IS challenging. However, some parents have experiences in the journey that are beyond the day-to-day keeping up with changing diapers, dealing with sibling squabbles, feeling like a taxi driver, keeping everyone in clean clothes, balancing the unbalancable budget, and maintaining some semblance of order in sacrament meeting. There seems to be an endless list of things to do and be as a parent. The parents to which I refer are those who have children who make choices that run against the most the fundamental commandments and demand the most serious consequences. Yes, these matters push parents way beyond the exhaustion of getting the laundry done and making it through the day. In addition to the physical and emotional drain, these parents have to deal with feelings of hopelessness, heartbreak, and public humiliation. I speak of parents whose children have joined the ranks of the criminal crowd and willful violators of the Lord's sexual code.

I want to share two true vignettes to illustrate my objective in this chapter. For obvious reasons, I will not disclose names or references that may identify the individuals concerned. I thank them for their permission to use their stories.

For Richard and Susan, the gospel was a fundamental part of their lives. Their family was central to their daily walk and talk. The temple was a centerpiece of their membership. Their covenants were an active part of who they were and how they lived. They had achieved a level of financial success in their lives and sought to be consecrational in the sharing of their blessings. Their dreams were on track to being fulfilled as their children were moving along the paths of Scouting, Eagle ranks, and Young Women medallions and toward missions, temple marriage, and building the same legacy of faith in the next generation. Everything seemed to be moving along in order.

With a missionary in the field and their daughter at a Church university, Susan one day sensed something was not right with that daughter. That unsettling feeling nudged her to get in her car and drive a few hours to see her daughter and determine what was wrong. While driving, a thought came to her that was so shocking she had to pull over to the side of the highway and calm her emotions. The Spirit communicated that her daughter was involved in same-sex attraction issues. When Susan finally arrived at her daughter's apartment and disclosed the feeling that had come to her in route, the feeling was confirmed. Difficult days followed. Heartbreak and shattered dreams for a bright future collapsed. One day, the same Spirit that bore the shocking message of the problem communicated another message: "You have to love her." Years have now passed. Her daughter has moved from the initial relationship to a new one. Richard and Susan show their love to their daughter. In the spirit of love, they have been able to communicate and have a close relationship with her. They and their daughter have an understanding—they cannot celebrate the union because of how firmly they believe in the doctrine of the family. Their relationship allows Richard and Susan to express their love to both their daughter and her partner while maintaining their stand on the side of their testimony of the "The Family: A Proclamation to the World" and the Lord's declarations. In Susan's own words:

> For me at this point there is a feeling of peace because of my trust in Heavenly Father and my faith in the Atonement. Of course I feel sorrow for her choices, but I do not suffer because of them.
>
> When I realized that I wasn't going to be able to "fix" her situation and that it was probably going to be long term, I felt that I had a choice to make. I could either shut her out of my life, or I could choose to love her and have her be a part of the family. If I shut her out of my life, there would be not further contact, and I would have lost the opportunity for my influence as well as the family's influence for her.
>
> In "The Family: A Proclamation to the World," it states that gender is eternal (*Ensign*, November 1995, 102). I firmly

believe this. As I have pondered about why my daughter has chosen her lifestyle, the Spirit taught me, "She has forgotten she is a daughter of a Heavenly Father who loves her." (If that sounds familiar it is because it is the first line of the Young Women Theme.) It is that simple. Since that realization, I have tried to take every opportunity by the way that I treat her to remind her that she *is* a daughter of a Heavenly Father who loves her, and we love her too. In dealing with this, I feel that I am navigating in "uncharted waters," but just like Lehi and his family, I have a Liahona (the Holy Ghost) to guide me. I do not need to fear. I can be happy!" (Used with permission)

Paul and Beth follow the pattern of the aforementioned couple. They too were like a poster family in the Church. Believing they could not have children, they chose to adopt. Not long after, they were blessed with the surprising birth of a child of their own. Moving forward in perfect sync, they raised their sons to be good and righteous boys. They taught them in their home, taking full advantage of Church and community programs to supplement their efforts. Like Richard, they too had to work, balance the checkbook, change dirty diapers, and help with homework. They had to settle sibling disputes and prod their children to clean their rooms, do their chores, and not put the cat in the dryer or pull the dog's hair. Their sons seemed to be on the right path in every visible way. On occasion, the older son exhibited rebellious attitudes and got in trouble at school. However, one day their dreams were shattered when the police arrived at their home to inform them that their oldest son had committed a serious crime. All that seemed nearly perfect, or at least normal, turned upside down. Jail time, hearings, court dates, and judgments followed. Correctional efforts, followed by a short season of good behavior, brought a repeat of even more serious crimes. Ultimately, prison time was deemed necessary and it was an obligation to live behind bars.

The story continues with a second chance, and there are challenging days ahead. Paul has said, "The Atonement and grace have helped me see my son as he really is. He has a good heart. The negative consequences of his poor choices will follow him for a long time, but in the eternities, I know he can enjoy every blessing every other repentant, perfected-in-Christ soul can, if he will. Healing has come from much prayer and meditation, and the light and knowledge from the Spirit have helped me see our son with new eyes, to see his heart and soul, and to be more trusting that our Heavenly Father's and our Savior's miraculous power will be manifest in his life."

These stories represent heavy challenges to parents who have borne them. They also teach how the Spirit, the Atonement, and grace can allow us to love the sinner, not the sin. They also testify of the Savior's love. Read the principle quote again, this time slow and deliberate. I have provided it in a bulleted format for emphasis on each point. Seek to understand Sister Okazaki's witness:

- "All of us face different family circumstances and home situations.
- All of us need strength in dealing with them.
- This strength comes from faith in the Savior's love and in the power of His Atonement.
- If we trustingly put our hand in the Savior's, we can claim the promise of the sacramental prayer to always have His Spirit with us.
- All problems are manageable with that strength, and all other problems are secondary in urgency to maintaining a strong spiritual life.
- Strengthen yourselves by seeking the source of true strength—the Savior.
- Come unto Him.
- He loves you.
- He desires your happiness.
- Make Him your strength, your daily companion, your rod, and your staff.
- Let Him comfort you.

- There is no burden we need bear alone.
- His grace compensates for our deficiencies." (Chieko Okazaki, "Strength in the Savior," *Ensign*, November 1993)

Parenting Self-Examination

1. Who do you know with similar challenges? How can you apply these principles to those situations?
2. How has the Atonement, the Spirit, and grace helped you work through challenges?
3. Write your testimony of the Savior. Take the opportunity to share that testimony vocally sometime soon.

Scriptures for Study

Bible Dictionary, "Grace," 697		1 Nephi 21:15–16
Jeremiah 31:15–16	D&C 138:58–59	Mormon 9:31
D&C 105:6	Romans 8:26	Matthew 11:28
Mosiah 27:14	D&C 100:1	Alma 33:11

A Parting Thought

Whether or not we can relate to these stories, it is my testimony that the Atonement, the Spirit, and grace are all fully operational and can help us in our "normal" daily challenges associated with being a parent. I know Jesus Christ is the practical and lifting answer, helping us during our parenting of small children, awkward preteens, teenagers, or struggling adult children. Sister Okazaki started our chapter, and I'd like to allow her to end it as well:

> Through the years, my circumstances have changed. I was a single woman, then the wife of a nonmember, then a partner in a temple sealing, a mother, a mother-in-law and grandmother, and now a widow. I have known the Savior's love in all of these circumstances. My own faith has been rewarded as I have felt

the Savior's presence and power in my home. (Chieko Okazaki, "Strength in the Savior," *Ensign*, November 1993)

> Remember: No recipes. Study. Self-examine. Do your best. Live worthy of the Holy Ghost. Pray that the Lord will touch your doings and consecrate them for the blessing and benefit of you, your children, and your grandchildren.

Principle 29

Yoked

"Happiness in family life is most likely to be achieved when founded upon the teachings of the Lord Jesus Christ. Successful marriages and families are established and maintained on principles of faith, prayer, repentance, forgiveness, respect, love, compassion, work, and wholesome recreational activities. By divine design, fathers are to preside over their families in love and righteousness and are responsible to provide the necessities of life and protection for their families. Mothers are primarily responsible for the nurture of their children. In these sacred responsibilities, fathers and mothers are obligated to help one another as equal partners. Disability, death, or other circumstances may necessitate individual adaptation. ("The Family: A Proclamation to the World," *Ensign*, November 1995, 102)

WHILE LIVING in Santiago, Chile, I became fascinated with something I learned about *la yunta*, or the yoke. Two oxen yoked together properly and trained to pull against the yoke in equal force actually produced the power and strength of up to six individual oxen. If there are only two oxen, how is it possible to produce the power of six individual animals? I also learned that two oxen pulling at even slightly different levels of strength, causing one side of the yoke to be a little weaker than the other, didn't even produce the power of one ox. Further, if one of the oxen was aggressive and more powerful than his yoke mate on the other side, it is possible that the more energetic and vigorous ox could lunge forward and break or injure the neck of the weaker in the pair.

How do two "equally yoked" oxen combine to create the power of six? Synergy. The dictionary definition is "the interaction or cooperation of two or more agents to produce a combined effect greater than the sum of their separate parts." Another simplistic definition is simply one plus on is three, or more. The power is in the quality and unity of the combination. I have to believe that no two oxen are identical in their strength. It requires give and take. As the pair work together, it is incumbent on the stronger of the two to adjust to the strength of the weaker so that together they can combine to create the maximum result. A stronger bullock who is unrestrained is actually a detriment to the production of power by working against the limited power of the weaker one. Totally unchecked, the intermittent surges of the stronger can produce tension so powerful on the neck and body of the other animal that it can be hurt or even incapacitated.

This metaphor became one of the common themes of our mission experience. It applied to companionships, working with local members or ecclesiastical leaders, and strengthening our capacity to give more in yoking ourselves to the Lord and Spirit. In the context of this book, it is also a powerful metaphor in helping us understand what can happen in marriage and parenting.

Paul taught, "Be ye not unequally yoked together" (2 Corinthians 6:14). Being equally yoked with our spouse in our efforts to be powerful parents is an effort that requires unity. Sometimes one needs to adjust a little and not be so forceful. This does not excuse the weaker to kick back and be a slacker. We always need to be doing our best and our part. However, the unified effort will always produce the best result.

Elder Neal A. Maxwell taught, "How can we value the family without valuing parenting? And how can we value parenting if we do not value marriage? How can there be 'love at home' without love in a marriage? So many selfish tugs draw fathers and mothers away from each other and away from their children" (" 'Take Especial Care of Your Family,' " *Ensign*, May 1994).

I remember a good woman came to me once and confided, "Bishop, I love my husband, and he loves me. Our marriage is not in trouble. But what do I do? He arises early each morning to go exercise before work. He's never around for family prayer or morning scripture study. He may briefly pause long enough when he comes home from the gym to turn on the TV to check sports scores while he gobbles down his Wheaties, and then he rushes out. He works hard and provides well for us, but when he comes home, he dresses down and relaxes in front of the TV to flip through the ESPN and other sports channels to find a game he wants to settle into for the rest of the evening. He usually requests his dinner be brought to him so he won't miss the game. Sometimes that's interrupted only by his Young Men calling in the ward or to play ball on a city recreation league team one night each week and with the ward team the other night. We never have dinner together as a family. We always have prayer as a family, but without him most of the time. What I worry about most is that our teenage son is following closely behind. What can I do? I've tried to adjust our family schedule to his, but I'm getting weary because everything revolves around some team's schedule, which is never consistent."

Sound familiar? It may not be sports. It could be friends, hobbies, fishing, hunting, boating, video gaming, or perhaps a job. And it's not just on the husband's side of the "yoke." I've seen the wife's side get lopsided in divided interests as well. The root of this and many associated problems is selfishness. When "everything revolves around me" takes a seat in the family circle, whether its parents or children, the family is impacted negatively.

There are few things that cause more challenges in the home

than the absence of unity or harmony. First, being unequally yoked as parents impacts and passes through to children. Not pulling together due to selfishness is a recipe for weak results in our parenting and has the potential for discord. When a husband or wife is insistent upon having everything his or her way, then contention is observed or felt by the children. They then choose one side or the other, or are left in confusion and will almost always seek comfort outside the family with peers or activities. If they do choose one side of unequally yoked parents, they learn that it provides to be an effective tool to manipulate parents to get their own selfish way—which adds yet another wedge of discord.

Children need to feel their home is a place of refuge from the world. Parents equally yoked supply that need. Being equally yoked as parents is necessary to add the Savior and the Holy Ghost into the yoke. Children will feel it, respect it, and find that they can add their strength to the yoke. Families yoked together in this way are a powerful force.

Parenting Self-Examination

1. Who are examples for you of "equally yoked" couples? What makes them that way?
2. How could you work to feel more "yoked"?
3. Are there any selfish behaviors on your side of the yoke? Will you change them?

Scriptures for Study

2 Corinthians 6:14   Mosiah 18:21   Colossians 2:2
John 17:21   3 Nephi 28:10   Ephesians 2:18–19

A Parting Thought

I love the metaphor of *la yunta*. Being yoked together, with each party doing their best, and adjusting our pull to match the team is actually fun and energizing. Elder Boyd K. Packer taught, "Parenthood is a sacred privilege, and depending upon faithfulness, it can be an eternal blessing. The ultimate end of all activity in the Church is that a man and his wife and their children can be happy at home" ("The Witness," *Ensign*, May 2014). Happy yoking!

> Remember: No recipes. Study. Self-examine. Do your best. Live worthy of the Holy Ghost. Pray that the Lord will touch your doings and consecrate them for the blessing and benefit of you, your children, and your grandchildren.

Principle 30

Come What May, and Love It

" 'Come what may, and love it.' . . . The next time you're tempted to groan, you might try to laugh instead. It will extend your life and make the lives of all those around you more enjoyable. . . . Seek for the eternal. You may feel singled out when adversity enters your life. You shake your head and wonder, 'Why me?' But the dial on the wheel of sorrow eventually points to each of us. At one time or another, everyone must experience sorrow. No one is exempt. . . . Understand the principle of compensation. The Lord compensates the faithful for every loss. That which is taken away from those who love the Lord will be added unto them in His own way. While it may not come at the time we desire, the faithful will know that every tear today will eventually be returned a hundredfold with tears of rejoicing and gratitude. . . . Put our trust in our Heavenly Father and His Son, Jesus Christ. . . . 'Come what may and love it.' " (Joseph B. Wirthlin, "Come What May, and Love It," *Ensign*, November 2008)

THIS QUOTE may not seem like it has a parenting focus, but I think it does. Joseph B. Wirthlin, in some measure, is the product of his parents. His mother taught him that one of the great practical foundations of life is living with whatever comes our way. Can you think of a greater gift you can give your children than to teach them to put their trust in Heavenly Father and His Son, Jesus Christ, and follow that by teaching them learn to embrace whatever experiences life provides them and to do their best with what they've graciously been given?

I too have been the benefactor of a mother who taught us well. Mom's "School of Life" was on Thursdays (bread baking day at the Christensen home). While I consumed a loaf of her extraordinary whole-wheat bread glazed with dripping butter and honey, Mother taught me through our life experiences (personally and as a family) to love whatever the Lord sees fit to give us.

She related to me over and over again the story of my hands. They are graced with large wax-like scars. "David, those scars are a reminder that Heavenly Father and Jesus Christ have the capacity to perform miracles in our lives." At age one, I fell on the hot coal-burning stove in our home and burned my hands so badly that amputation was a primary consideration at one point. Prayers, a priesthood blessing, and the combined faith of many preserved my hands and have given me a wonderful reminder and token of Heavenly Father's tender mercy. Instead of hiding my scars, Mother taught me to embrace them.

She also often reminded me of the time when I was three and my older brother and two older sisters contracted polio. One of my sisters, Jan, lived the rest of her life with a crutch, a leg brace, and limited use of her hands and arms. Mother taught me that those trying and difficult days were, in part, the reason our family was so close and our family ties so strong. Later in our lives, Apostle LeGrand Richards gave her a blessing and confirmed my mother's wisdom and teaching by indicating that Jan and her challenges were in fact crowning jewels in our family.

These stories, along with others such as her and Dad losing the family farm twice and living through the Depression, add depth to our family legacy. Mother set a pattern to know in my mind and to feel deeply in the innermost part of my heart about trusting in God. She taught me that those who are faithful and doing their best by moving their feet will be blessed by Heavenly Father. She taught me that He only bestows blessings. She helped me to see that our adversities are, in fact, invitations to grow and are designed to bless us.

Mother skillfully taught me keys to understanding the ups and downs in life and to credit God for all things that are a part of His agenda for developing us. She taught me the essence of scriptural testimony.

Lehi said to his son Jacob, who was born in the early days of their eight years in the wilderness, "Thou knowest the greatness of God; and he shall consecrate thine afflictions for thy gain. Wherefore, thy soul shall be blessed" (2 Nephi 2:2–3). Nephi added, "O how great the holiness of our God! For he knoweth all things, and there is not anything save he knows it" (2 Nephi 9:20). "But behold, all things have been done in the wisdom of him who knoweth all things" (2 Nephi 2:24).

I am eternally grateful to my mother for those Thursday afternoons at the kitchen table, not only ingesting her bread but also internalizing lessons I needed to understand. Those lessons have blessed me through a handful of major challenges of my own and helped me keep in check the great days of our lives—always crediting the Lord of all blessings.

We must ask ourselves: What are we teaching our children? What lessons are we giving them to help get them through the hard days of adolescence? Through a full-time mission? To repair the little rips and tears that can enter into their own marriages and parenting trials?

PRINCIPLE 30

Parenting Self-Examination

1. Considering the present age of your children, what have you done thus far to teach them the essence of Elder Wirthlin's message in the quote for this principle? Read it again. Ask yourself: What am I doing? What more can I do?
2. Scan back through your own life and make a short list of the useful things your parents taught you. Which of them would you like to pass on to the next generation?
3. Write your thoughts in your journal. Perhaps they will be helpful to you in the future or inspire future readers.

Scriptures for Study

| 2 Nephi 2:2–3 | 2 Nephi 9:20 | D&C 121:7–8 |
| John 3:16 | Job 19:25–26 | Romans 8:28 |

A Parting Thought

We can help our children understand that thorns, thistles, briars, and aggravating weeds are a part of life. Teaching them how to reframe those challenging times and see them as blessings is one of the most useful lessons we can pass on. Elder Wirthlin said of his mother, "'Come what may, and love it.' . . . I think she may have meant that every life has peaks and shadows and times when it seems that the birds don't sing and the bells don't ring. Yet in spite of discouragement and adversity, those who are happiest seem to have a way of learning from difficult times, becoming stronger, wiser, and happier as a result" ("Come What May, and Love It," *Ensign*, November 2008).

Remember: No recipes. Study. Self-examine. Do your best. Live worthy of the Holy Ghost. Pray that the Lord will touch your doings and consecrate them for the blessing and benefit of you, your children, and your grandchildren.

Principle 31

How Will They Remember Me?

"Our children will remember us by our example. . . . We, as parents, have the privilege and the responsibility of teaching gospel principles by our example and testimony to our loved ones. . . . The calling of father or mother is sacred and carries with it great significance. One the greatest privileges and responsibilities given to us is that of being a parent—helping to bring to earth a child of God and having the sacred responsibility to love, care, and guide children back to Heavenly Father. In many ways earthly parents represent their Heavenly Father in the process of nurturing, loving, caring, and teaching children. Children naturally look to their parents to learn the characteristics of their Heavenly Father. (Robert D. Hales, "How Will Our Children Remember Us?" *Ensign*, November 1993)

FOR MUCH of my life, I've associated funerals with death and closing. I've learned that, in reality, funerals are about living. Funerals are a time when life is featured and celebrated. Paying our respects is a chance for the living to remember. Remembering and commemorating life is what we do at a funeral. As I ponder and consider the memories of family members in a funeral setting, I'm inspired to consider what memories I am building.

I love the lyrics to one of the hymns we often sing at these celebrations of life (funerals). For the purpose of this chapter and its message, I have substituted the word *parents* for *friends*. In the context of its message, it's a perfect anthem for answering the question, "How will my children remember me?" Contemplate the power of its message from the following verse:

> What greater gift dost thou bestow,
> What greater goodness can we know

> Than Christlike [parents], whose gentle ways
> Strengthen our faith, enrich our days.
> ("Each Life That Touches Ours for Good," *Hymns*, no. 293)

A mission president has the opportunity to conduct a lot of interviews with missionaries under his direction. Many times those encounters included some discussion about parents and grandparents. Most missionaries recounted with fondness the blessings they received from their parents, grandparents, and other special individuals. Frequently, remembering the deeds, examples, and love of their parents caused missionaries to become emotional with a profound sense of gratitude.

Someone once said, "Memory is the mother of feeling." Remembering the positive and heartfelt influence of parents, grandparents, and other loved ones creates a special feeling of gratitude and becomes an energizing force in our lives.

Let's ponder the question given by Elder Hales that goes along with his quote at the beginning of this chapter: "I find myself asking the question, 'How will my children remember me?' How will they remember you?" ("How Will Our Children Remember Us?" *Ensign*, November 1993).

I invited others to respond to that question. Perhaps what they remember about their parents will give us some direction as to what we hope our children will remember about us.

- "I remember my mother used to always read to us. There was something about her voice, snuggling next to her and listening to her read, that lives on today twenty-three years later."
- "Dad was always looking for an opportunity to teach us something about life using the symbols created by Heavenly Father: leaves, wind, ants, water, sun, flowers, bees, and clouds. How did he know I'd remember these things all my life?"
- "I remember catching my parents on their knees praying together many times. One time it was late at night. I listened to what they prayed about and was surprised that they prayed

about me and my brothers and sisters. That image of their silhouette in the dark, kneeling in prayer about me, has sustained me many times in my life."

- "We always had a vacation we planned months in advance. Mom and Dad knew that half the fun of a vacation is in planning, dreaming, and talking about it."
- "Family home evening lasted from 6:00 p.m. to midnight every Monday evening. The lesson lasted for fifteen or twenty minutes, but the evening was set aside for our family, and we knew it."
- "I remember the smell of cinnamon rolls and the tradition of seeing my parents intently taking notes while we listened to general conference. Dad used to say that as much as he loved Christmas, the two greatest weekends on earth were the first weeks of April and October."
- "I remember lying on the bed of the trampoline looking up at the stars and having Dad tell fantasy stories where I was always the hero and nice guy."
- "We had family prayer twice a day everyday."
- "Dinner time was family time. Even if for only twenty minutes, we ate dinner together every night at six. We'd talk about the day, laugh, and sometimes get into longer discussions. Sometimes when younger brothers would leave to go do chores or play, it was a time I knew I could hang around and talk to my dad and mom."
- "Every Saturday we did family 'work in the yard morning,' followed by an awesome breakfast. We lived in a warm climate, so work had to be done early, and then the rest of the day was family playtime."
- "I remember my parents sometimes talking about not being able to afford a particular activity or vacation. Then they would begin to figure out a way to do it, saying, 'Life is all about memories. This will be something important to create memories. Let's find a way to do it.' Other times they would

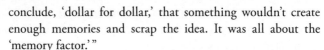

conclude, 'dollar for dollar,' that something wouldn't create enough memories and scrap the idea. It was all about the 'memory factor.'"

- "I could tell that my parents loved having Church callings and loved to serve. Mom would take me with her to deliver a casserole to someone in our ward. She would always let me carry something and explain how we bless and help each other."

- "Sometimes I missed my dad at church because he was always in a bishopric, on the high council, or in the stake presidency. But I always knew that he was committed to helping others and would put the Lord and us first as best he could."

- "My parents were the meanest parents in the world! They wouldn't let us buy anything we wanted. They made us get jobs as soon as we could work. They made us pay for our own clothes when we could. They helped us set up a budget and a savings plan and always reminded us about our tithing. They were the meanest and bestest parents anyone could ever have."

- "When I think of my parents, I see they were yoked together in every way. *Together* is the word I think of. Together, supportive, and unified in discipline, fun, and planning. I love that."

- "My mom had a hard life. As a simple mom, she was faithful and steady, and she loved us. I will forever be grateful."

- "My dad was a hard worker and thought school sports were a waste of time. But he was always at my games if he could be. I heard his voice over all the others cheering me on."

Parenting Self-Examination

1. If you were to write a list of what you hope your children will remember about you when they speak at your funeral, what would you include?
2. What are three most important things you hope your kids will remember about you?
3. How are you doing in those areas? What are two things you

can do consistently, beginning today, to set patterns you hope your children will remember?

Scriptures for Study

Helaman 5:6–9, 12	Proverbs 10:7	Alma 36:17
Alma 46:12	Alma 48:17–19	Genesis 41:37–41

A Parting Thought

A celebration of life, the whole life. Some of the tender stories shared are of when the person was less than perfect. Some of our passing heroes have learned lessons the hard way. But the greatest celebrations are for those who loved us and recognized the gifts God gave them. Their lives reflect the Savior. May we always be found asking ourselves, "How can I act and be a parent who is trying to be like the Savior? What will I do today?"

Remember: No recipes. Study. Self-examine. Do your best. Live worthy of the Holy Ghost. Pray that the Lord will touch your doings and consecrate them for the blessing and benefit of you, your children, and your grandchildren.

About the Author

DAVID A. Christensen's love for present-day prophets was sparked as a young returned missionary student at Brigham Young University when he took the religion class "Teachings of the Living Prophets." He has a testimony of listening to and seeking to follow those who are charged with helping us understand the Lord's will and direction in our lives. David has taught the same course, "Teaching of the Living Prophets," for over two decades at BYU–I. He sought to pass on that same testimony and love for the counsel given by living prophets to missionaries when he presided over the Chile Santiago North Mission, the Guatemala MTC, and in his service as stake president and bishop.

He counts his eight children and growing number of grandchildren as his most important converts, and his best friend and wife, Deena Bond Christensen, his eternal companion.